Taj Mahal
Multiple Narratives

First published in 2017

Om Books International

Corporate & Editorial Office
A-12, Sector 64, Noida 201 301
Uttar Pradesh, India
Phone: +91 120 477 4100
Email: editorial@ombooks.com
Website: www.ombooksinternational.com

Sales Office
107, Ansari Road, Darya Ganj, New Delhi 110 002, India
Phone: +91 11 4000 9000
Fax: +91 11 2327 8091
Email: sales@ombooks.com
Website: www.ombooks.com

Editor: Dipa Chaudhuri
Design: Alpana Khare Graphic Design
Picture research: Amita Baig, Rahul Mehrotra, Alpana Khare & Ipshita Mitra

ISBN: 978-93-83202-02-7

10 9 8 7 6 5 4 3 2 1

Printed in India

Taj Mahal
Multiple Narratives

Amita Baig and Rahul Mehrotra

Om Books International

Contents

Preceding page, top: The inspiration behind Shahjahan's grand monuments was Mumtaz Mahal, his third and most favoured wife, who died giving birth to her 14th child.

Facing page: This painting from the famous Petersburg album assembled in Iran in 1750 shows the Mughal Emperor Shahjahan (top left) with his sons Aurangzeb (top right) and Dara Shikoh (bottom left). It is richly decorated with a floral border, and the calligraphy identifies the family (except the person to the bottom right).

Prologue
Engaging with the Taj Mahal

Taj Mahal: Multiple Narratives grew out of the many years we spent visiting the Taj Mahal together, and each time, we were more fascinated by the yet many more stories that emerged than we had ever imagined. Sometimes, these emerged through scholarship we read and engaged with, and sometimes by just listening to folklore from the numerous people we met during our visits to this iconic site, or from the wonderful graffiti we saw on the walls of the different buildings around the Taj Mahal – some dating back over a century.

A few years ago, as we left the Taj Mahal from the Fatehpuri Gate where Indian visitors queue in silence for hours in the scorching sun, waiting to enter and pay their respects at the mausoleum, we knew that there was a larger story to be told, especially in our cultural context, including stories that embraced the city and those who contributed to the culture that could create a monument of such incredible ambition.

In India, we have grown up listening to stories that surround the Taj Mahal – of masons being blinded so as to never imagine a rival monument; of the Black Taj that was never realised; of the cruelty that emperors heaped upon their subjects, and more. It was partly our desire to demystify these stories that broadened our own ambitions about what to capture and narrate – all in the belief that these multiple narratives would not only enrich the visitors' experience but ground the monument much more squarely in the local, popular imagination.

In the year 2000, we were invited by Tata's Indian Hotels Company (IHCL) to develop a conservation management plan for the Taj Mahal – a dream project for us as professionals engaged with conservation in India. IHCL's mandate was that only the best

Below: This early 1860 watercolour of the Taj Mahal is by an anonymous artist travelling through Agra, who not only captured the lushness of trees around the monument but also artfully included the British concept of an ideal landscape with a lawn in 'front' of the mausoleum.

was acceptable for the Taj Mahal; they were truly exceptional in their breadth of vision. The late Ravi Dubey and Shirin Baltiwala from IHCL drove this, as a partnership between the corporate sector and government agencies was yet untested and tenuous.

The entire process of our engagement involved research, documentation, workshops with experts and the officials of the Archaeological Survey of India (ASI), and sometimes, spontaneous trips to contemplate solutions. We believed that working on the Taj Mahal was such a privilege that it would be inappropriate to have individual names associated with something as sublime and enduring as the Taj, so we established a collective – The Taj Mahal Conservation Collaborative (TMCC) as it came to be popularly known in Agra

Facing page above: This lithographic print dated 1883 from a pamphlet called Ziyarat Al Arab, A Pilgrimage to India, *is an invaluable record of how the monument was still perceived as a sacred site even a hundred years after it was built.*

Taj Be ka Roya Agera ka.

over the five or six years we worked there. We remain deeply indebted to our colleagues Dr. Priyaleen Singh, Annabel Lopez, Arup Sarbadhikary, Navin Piplani and Tara Sharma, as also to the many young architects from RMA Architects who participated at different times and formed the core TMCC team, and who embraced the ideals and worked with us for many years, long after our formal obligations as consultants had ended. However, our commitment to the Taj Mahal never did. We had invested an immense amount of time in the hope that the many ideas we had collectively generated would, in the interest of the future of this breathtaking monument, be realised.

The signing of a Memorandum of Understanding (MOU) between one of India's premiere industrial houses and the ASI in 2000, was a master stroke envisioning public-private partnership, then at a very nascent stage in India's emerging economy. That Government responded to the offer of partnership so readily was also a first. It was a project ripe with promise, with opportunity to establish benchmarks for excellence, and for the first time in India, a World Heritage Site was viewed in its totality. Almost at its inception, it was agreed that a Site Management Plan would 'front end' the project as it would establish principles and strategies for the future management of the Taj Mahal as a whole, and for credible methodologies of decision-making. It would provide through its appropriate application, a forum for discussion, which would assist both the ASI and the local authorities in managing a most complex site, given that it came under the purview of the Supreme Court Judgement of 1994. This meant that all conservation proposals or any infrastructure improvement needed to be vetted by the Supreme Court monitoring committee appointed to review the Taj Mahal and its surroundings. Thus the creation of a site management plan would also act as a framework for the committee to understand the reasons and relevance of any proposal, given the broader gamut of issues surrounding the Taj Mahal.

With this sound background, research was undertaken to assess available data. The Taj Mahal is, without doubt, one of the most intensely studied sites in the world. For example, an alarmist report by a structural engineer visiting the Taj Mahal in 1985 declaring it to be at risk, resulted in a slew of studies, national and international, by those who thought otherwise; the Supreme Court case also heralded environmental studies of significant nature. So the first and major exercise was to create

Above: The 1870 painting of the Taj Mahal by Nicholas Chevalier shows the garden somewhat overgrown. Nonetheless, the water channels and fountains are still functional. It is clear in this painting that the char bagh complex had been transformed into a recreational space.

Below: In the 20th century, the Taj Mahal became one of the most intensively studied monuments, with a proliferation of drawings, paintings and plans. Drawings such as these are critical tools for conservators today, providing clues on how the building was constructed, and the complexity of its construction. Many such details are still being discovered.

a bibliography of research and publications on the Taj, which would serve as the basic resource work for all consultants working in TMCC. This was followed by a compilation of all the scientific research and study undertaken on the monument, and then by a comprehensive timeline of the conservation work done by the ASI since its inception.

We owe our gratitude to the global experts whom we invited to guide our deliberations. The late Sir Bernard Feilden, the patriarch of conservation, taught us the value of being contemporary in our decisions. Noted Taj scholar Prof. Ebba Koch, and James Westcoat's incredible knowledge of the field remains a core guide. Their work on the Taj has been truly motivating for us. Milo C. Beach's depth of knowledge

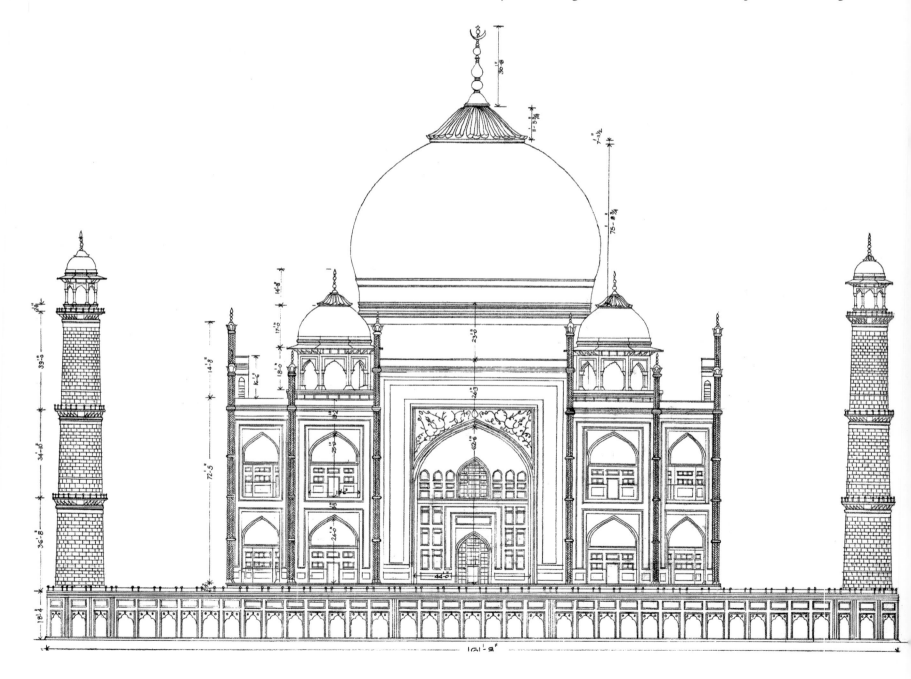

and sensitivity was an immense inspiration, as were Senake Bandranayake, Marukh Tarapore and Martand Singh – all of whom benchmark excellence and infuse immense passion in what they do. The Getty Institute and World Monuments Fund provided institutional partnership which was invaluable to our work.

Following the guidance of the first international experts' meeting in September 2001, the project moved forward very quickly, with multiple threads fanning out to different aspects of the site. The ASI identified the two *khwasspuras* as potential visitor centres to address this lacuna as well as resolve pending visitor management problems. Once historian Prof. Ebba Koch confirmed this was, in fact, their original use, it became clear that this was an ideal project as it was set away from the mausoleum and easily accessible to the public. The project was also fast-tracked as it became apparent that if the gardens and central concourse were to be restored, a very clear visitor-management plan needed to be operational in order to not disrupt India's most visited site. Tourism management was also prioritised as visitors' experience was largely seen to be cumbersome and hardly did the Taj any credit.

Visitor movement within the site was also carefully studied in order to reduce pressure on the central concourse and develop less visited buildings within the complex. This led to the induction of signage and site information as well as preliminary assessments to upgrade and improve the museum and the largely disused building opposite also known as the *Naubat Khana*. With the two *Naubat Khanas* more fully utilised, visitor dispersal within the site could be assured.

The Taj Mahal is a large site covering more than 16 hectares within its walls and, therefore, state-of-the-art data management systems also became essential in order to provide easily accessible information. It was our view that with proper facilities, management and an upgraded visitor experience, the public's relationship with the monument would become more responsible as well.

Particularly satisfying and simultaneously intriguing were the discoveries about the gardens, led by the TMCC expert, Dr. Priyaleen Singh. The intense research to recreate the logic of what the orginal gardens might have been was something that fascinated us as a team. The idea that the garden was so central to the design intent of the Taj Mahal, and had been altered, thus undermining its fundamental quality, was a challenge for us. For, to imagine the sense of weightlessness of this white

Above and top: In the 1990s, excavations on the opposite side of the Taj Mahal yielded the remains of Mehtab Bagh. Above the ground, a single burj *was clearly visible but the excavations unearthed a huge octagonal pond, water systems and the remains of a walled garden, all of which gave rise to new interpretations of the Taj Mahal's grand plan.*

13

Below: The painting of a youth and a singing girl from the manuscript of Jami, Baharistan (Gardens of Spring), dated 1595 was commissioned by Emperor Akbar and showcases the importance of gardens in Mughal life.

The char bagh offers immense opportunities for research ranging from imaginations of jannat to the walled pleasure gardens with their finely nuanced flora and fauna.

Facing page: Humayun pensively holds a sarpech, a jewelled turban ornament that Mughal emperors bestowed on a family member indicating either lineage or a favour granted. Paintings such as these reflect the oasis of beauty and order that the Mughals created for themselves.

Bottom: This painting of a noble woman, seated on a golden chair, drinking wine and waited upon by an attendant in the midst of trees and wildlife, clearly indicates that women of the court who shared the emperor's fascinations, lived life to the full.

monument (alluding to white cloth stretched over a framework) floating in a paradise garden, made us rally together to establish a narrative that would communicate this idea. Thus, to articulate with evidence the original garden that concealed the base of the Taj Mahal, became, for a while, the central mission of our work. To establish the inauthenticity of the present garden layout was no easy task. It fundamentally challenged not only the world's imagination about the Taj Mahal and its setting but it also unsettled the status quo on the preservation of the monument. The Taj Mahal, we realised, has come to be imagined with the garden in its present form – and a difficult image to reverse as it is the image by which the world knows and imagines this incredible monument. Thus, we felt that the time was not right perhaps to question and challenge the perceived authenticity of the gardens and their relationship to the Taj Mahal. Strategically, therefore, we decided it should, for now, take on the form of an exhibition in the visitor centres, with the hope that another generation would have the confidence and the will to reverse the beautification that Lord Curzon had imposed on the Taj Mahal at the turn of the 20th century.

Over the next few years, regular site meetings were held and work proceeded perhaps slower than one would have liked, but also in the early stages of the programme, the public-private partnership was untested, and the Taj Mahal drew far more attention than any other monument in the country. Each step, therefore, was carefully calibrated, trying to dovetail new knowledge systems.

Working at the Taj Mahal threw up new problems and opportunities almost each day. All the consultants suddenly became aware of the sensitivities of working with security risks; architects making measured drawings would suddenly face the muzzle of a gun. We faced challenges of removing cows from the disused cowshed as the *khwasspuras* had come to be called; a fractured truce prevailed between the local authorities and the ASI, resulting in impossible site management; the absence of in-depth research on Mughal gardens, water contamination in the River Yamuna resulted in borewells being sunk to provide water to the Taj's ingenious water channel system. Proposals to restore the pathways were halted as discussions ensued on the importance of retaining the original masons' signature marks, skilfully etched into the stones, that would be lost if the damaged stones were replaced.

In the summer of 2004, as work on the Taj progressed slowly and surely, an alarming report appeared in the newspapers:

14

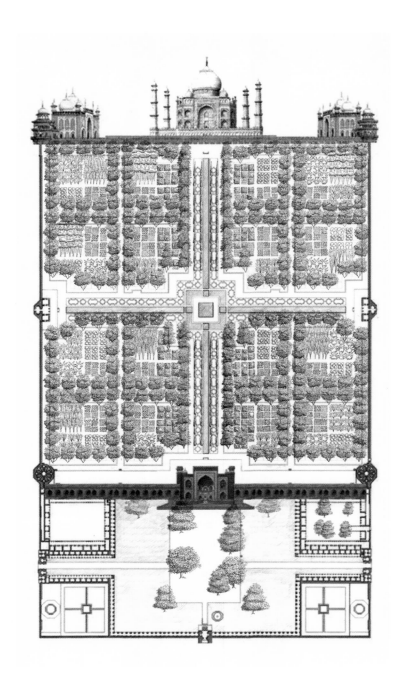

Above: In the early 20th century, the untended gardens of the Taj Mahal were believed to diminish the view of the Taj, and were replaced with lawns as the perfect foil to the pristine monument. As part of the Taj Mahal Conservation Collaborative's engagement with the Taj, Priyaleen Singh constructed drawings to recreate the spirit of the gardens, replete with all their nuances.

the riverbed below the Agra Fort, designated a World Heritage Site because it is 'inextricably linked to the Taj Mahal', was being reclaimed for development, including a shopping mall to attract tourists. Although construction in the Taj Buffer Zone is prohibited within the 500-metre radius of the Taj Mahal, in a curious twist of terminology, the reclaimed riverbed came to be known as the Taj Heritage Corridor. It became the *cause célèbre* of the year, with the Central Government pitted against the State to safeguard the monument's precincts. The corridor was abandoned as the Supreme Court stepped in with even more restrictions and strictures upon both State and Central Governments, rendering both completely helpless.

The visitor centres in the *khwasspuras*, which instead of being completed as endorsed not only by IHCL's experts but also by UNESCO's World Heritage Centre, became embroiled in the Supreme Court's prohibitions. In an odd system of decision-making, the fate of conservation and adaptive reuse projects was to be determined by judges and lawyers rather than specialists and experts who mediate strategies such as these, based on internationally accepted norms and guidelines.

In 2008, the Parliamentary Standing Committee asked for a solution to what had become enormous visitor management issues, with crowds waiting 3 to 4 hours in the sun as security systems had become cumbersome rather than efficient. IHCL once again responded to the ASI and completely redesigned the visitor centres and a new but significantly larger visitor management facility was proposed and presented at a special bench hearing in 2010. The judges were unanimous in their approval of these revisions. For a number of reasons, several ideas and plans floated by TMCC are yet to be carried through in the absence of the broader armature of a cohesive vision – a drive and motivation to contribute to safeguarding the Taj Mahal, not as a marble edifice but one which has myriad secrets and stories yet to be told, both mystical and enduring.

After many years, we decided to do this book to capture at least some of the stories that surround this great monument that inspired us. But more importantly, the book showed us how richer narratives could actually result in a deeper engagement with its conservation and continuing relevance in the city of Agra. Even though we are deeply aware of the immense scholarship which has preceded this book, we pressed ahead in the hope that new readings of the Taj Mahal would only enrich its imagination.

For us there have been three seminal reference books on the Taj Mahal that have influenced the evolution and structure of this book. To know the Taj we studied Ebba Koch's *The Complete Taj Mahal* published in 2006, which interrogated the building from different perspectives and a multitude of scholarly accounts as well as interpreted its aesthetics through the study of symbolism. To understand the Taj Mahal W. Begley and Z.A. Desai's book *Taj Mahal: The Illumined Tomb* published in 1989 is invaluable for its scholarly interpretations of the traditions and culture of the Mughal era. Lastly, Elizabeth Moynihan's research in 1996 in her book *The Moonlight Garden: New Discoveries at The Taj* opened up for us a completely altered perspective of the grand plan through the introduction of a sophisticated and deeply researched narrative on the Mehtab Bagh. Our effort has been to establish the simultaneous value of these three different narratives and synthesise these to construct perhaps a more inclusive interpretation of this stunningly beautiful monument. Inspired by these three works and with research from many other scholars in published papers, monographs and our own work on the ground we have developed the structure of multiple narratives which we hope will enrich how all of us view the Taj Mahal.

We are deeply grateful to Sulaiman Mahmoodabad, Syeda Imam and Muzzaffar Ali for their generous guidance on how we structured our interpretation. Richard Engelhardt's capacity to distill and his sensitivity to the Asian context was an invaluable guide. We are so thankful to Ritika Khanna, our valued research associate who was tireless in referencing our stories and searching the archives, and to Ayesha Mehrotra for having compiled the bibliography. We would like to acknowledge the Canadian Centre for Architecture, Montreal, for giving us access to their archives rich with images of the Taj Mahal, and for providing the luxury of their facililties to collate our thoughts.

We extend our profound gratitude to our friend Serga Nadler who has so generously shared her late husband Daniel's photographs. These photographs reflect not only Dan's sensitivity to architecture, but much more – his love for India. His photographs have greatly enriched this book.

Charles Gracias, Navin Piplani, Vineet Diwarkar, Development and Research Organisation for Nature, Arts and Heritage (DRONAH), Gurmeet Rai, Annabel Lopez, Rajesh Vohra and Romil Seth, have all been very generous in sharing their invaluable photographs which showcase the multiple narratives.

Above and top: Seen through the trees from its southern entrance, now popularly known as the main gate, the Taj Mahal would appear mystically through the foliage, and not reveal itself in its entirety almost until one was halfway to its platform.

Following pages: This 18th-century image of the Taj is more an imaginative rendition as piers, decks and embellishments erode the purity of symmetry and design.

منظرہ تاج گنج سمت دریا سے

Most of all, we owe a profound debt of gratitude to the Archaeological Survey of India whose records and information have been a vital resource for us. We have been especially particular to use material and resources available in India and have, to the best of our ability, been faithful to that. We are very grateful to the Directors General of the ASI over the last decade, most notably Mr. K.N. Srivastav, for their cooperation and engagement in our work. We especially thank Dr. Rakesh Tewari, Director General, ASI, Mr. Shharat Sharma, Dr. B.R. Mani and Mr. Janhwij Sharma, all of whom have given us access to the Taj's many hidden secrets.

We owe our deepest thanks to the Superintendent Archaeologists and officers of the Agra Circle – over the years as each one, including Dr. Bhuvan Vikram, enriched our knowledge and understanding of the Taj Mahal. Special thanks are due to Mr. P.B.S. Sengar, Dr. Dayalan and Mr. N.K. Pathak who have been very generous in sharing their knowledge and their treasured archives which we relied upon extensively. We are truly appreciative of Mr. Munazzar Ali who, for many years, was Conservation Assistant at the Taj and lovingly cared for the monument, and with whom we have worked closely, discovering its many secrets along the way. We remain deeply grateful to our many friends and colleagues at the Archaeological Survey of India, whose committment and devotion to the preservation of India's heritage, especially the Taj Mahal, often remains undervalued. Om Books International has been tremendously supportive and we are truly grateful, especially to Ajay Mago and Dipa Chaudhuri who so readily agreed to showcase our multiple narratives. Dipa has been an amazing editor, working her way through multiple iterations of our text and we are indebted to her meticulous work. Ipshita Mitra has been tireless in sourcing images which have so enriched the book, and we thank her profusely. Alpana Khare has shared our love affair with the Taj Mahal over many years, discovering its myriad secrets with us. Her shared passion reflects in this book that she has designed so elegantly.

Amita Baig and Rahul Mehrotra

Introduction
Multiple Narratives

To tell the story of the Taj Mahal is a daunting task; to tell it anew is perhaps even more so. Yet in India, no building is comparable in concept, beauty, scale and ambition, and no story about it can ever be complete. The Taj Mahal in its white marble glory stands out, a symbol of love, of empire and of an emperor's unyielding determination to construct *jannat* or paradise on earth. Each of its multiple narratives which try to reconstruct the whole, has a nuance that elicits new interpretations. In *Myths of the Taj Mahal and a New Theory of its Symbolic Meaning* (1972),[1] Wayne Begley makes a persuasive argument that this was not a mere mausoleum. It was far more symbolic and had profound and ambitious dimensions. Writings on the Taj Mahal vary from the flowery, almost obsequious court records, to latter accounts of 19th- and 20th-century travel writers, influenced by the new liberal and rational discourse, emerging socio-political thinkers, and democratisation imbued with more measured interpretations bordering on the prosaic. But never before, or since, has a tomb of this stature been built for an empress, and certainly Shah Jahan's own ancestors were far more modestly interred.

However, even as we venture to interpret what Shah Jahan envisioned, why he didn't plan for his own mortality still remains a mystery. It was certainly this absence which gave rise to the legend of the Black Taj across the river where Mehtab Bagh stands. Perhaps, he was so inebriated with power that he believed he was infallible, or in all likelihood, despite their rivalry, he believed his sons would provide for him. Maybe time simply ran out, since after building Shahjahanabad in Delhi, he was imprisoned in Agra until his end.

A descendant of Timur on the one side, and of Rajputs on the other, Shah Jahan was born of a mother who was a Suryavanshi – believed to have descended from the sun – from Marwar. Undoubtedly influenced by his twin lineage, and unlike Akbar who dabbled in the possibility of a new and overarching faith under his leadership, Shah Jahan possibly appropriated the paradigm of merging the spiritual and temporal from Hindu rulers. In fact, he often deviated from the puritanism of the *ulema* as he was undoubtedly influenced by his Hindu lineage as well.

Mughal emperors were great devotees of Sufi saints and even Babur circumambulated Nizamuddin Auliya's grave in Delhi before moving to Agra where he made his palace garden. Akbar built Fatehpur Sikri, following his devotions to Salim Chisti, an influence that stayed with his sons and grandson. Several scholars are of the opinion that the Taj Mahal was a monument which reflected the zenith of the Mughal Empire, and was patronised by a man possibly experimenting with the hereafter, with perhaps a touch of xenophobia. The emperor would remain the unrivalled emperor of the world, and explore a dimension in which emperor and God became one, each a reflection of the other.

Shah Jahan only ever saw the tomb from the riverfront as he travelled by barge from his fort. His vision, therefore, was circumscribed by a perceptual map, one rarely seen by the visitor and one that potentially offers new imaginations of the monument. If one were to see the Taj Mahal through the emperor's eyes, one would realise that the northern wall along the waterfront is the only external wall so richly embellished, clearly in recognition that this was the emperor's entrance. He would have arrived by barge, below the *takht*, his perspective of the Taj Mahal determined by this vantage point. Furthermore, maps of the time show the projection at the Taj Mahal using the river, not the *char bagh*, as the central point, thus clearly indicating that all perspective of the time used the river as the point of arrival, the centre of the larger complex of the Taj Mahal.

Equally, this site expresses the duality of the emperor's ideas, one so powerful that little stood between him and the unknown – perhaps a power which even drove him to create, rather simulate, the unknown. Each element provides an allegory of this duality – from the royal to the spiritual, the ruler and the *ulema*, the emperor and the commoner, perhaps even 'heaven' and earth. The metaphor extends throughout the complex and is most

Above: Genealogy was vital to the Mughals in establishing the lineage and relationships from the great Timur to the more fragmented Mughal dynasty in India where the position of an emperor was often secured through the ruthless removal of his closest relatives and contenders. Genealogical charts such as this one were often prepared more for a display of brotherhood than out of any sincere feeling of fraternal fealty.

Facing page: This 18th-century painting by Goverdhan establishes the unquestionable position of the emperor, holding his crown to possibly entice his sons who would be eligible to be seated by his side. Below them, the courtiers wait on the emperor and his sons. The canopy and carpets are as elaborately woven as the royal umbrellas.

Preceding pages: The emperor only ever approached the Taj Mahal by boat from the fort, which defined his perspective of the monument. The richly embellished façade befits the royal entrance at a time when the pristine waters of the Yamuna would have flowed alongside.

Right: This early painting of the Taj is from an Indian and Persian collection, and depicts a substantial stand of mature trees providing a lush foil to the marble monument. There are, however, three water channels instead of one. The idea of the char bagh, barely tended, is visible, nonetheless, in this painting.

Left: In this miniature with noblemen seated in a char bagh, *the garden is presented from a diagonal perspective, with a balustrade at the lower end. At the rear of the garden is a high wall and to the left is a doorway with an arched entrance. The water channels are bordered by a mass of small flowering plants. In the* char bagh *is a variety of trees, including cypress, banana palms, flowering and leafy trees, interspersed with flowering plants. Birds are shown flying between or perched on the trees in the background. This is an excellent rendering of a Mughal garden, especially with details of the plants around the main frame.*

clearly captured in the calligraphy on the *pishtaq*s, leaving little doubt that the entire plan was based on the idea of the hereafter, the rest taking creativity and architecture to such a level that no one would ever surpass it or even question its symbolism. The Taj Mahal is undoubtedly conceived as a sacred space. Perhaps, Shah Jahan was conceited enough to experiment with the duality of the ideals of building the mythical place – an imagined connection between heaven and earth? The entire concept reflects this duality, the sense of reaching for the unreachable, creating *jannat*. Each element is so fantastical that, in fact, it is just that.

In *Taj Mahal: Multiple Narratives*, we have tried to restrict ourselves to using the word '*jannat*' to distinguish it from paradise, a Christian interpretation of the 'unknown'. The Quran provides details of the eternal garden 'in whose hollows brooks flow'[2]. Yet, there is no precise guideline for how this is to be done. It is an allegorical description with trees providing eternal shade, many springs flowing with water, milk, honey, wine, and other rewards awaiting the faithful. There are numerous interpretations of *jannat* as scholars worldwide attempt to deconstruct the opaque allegories.

The word '*jannat*' is of Arabic origin and paradise is perhaps derived from the Persian '*firdaus*'. The translation into a garden was undoubtedly influenced by the arid landscape in which the rulers or nobility lived, where a walled retreat with water and shade was undoubtedly a luxury.

From the Maghreb to India, the walled garden provided a micro-climate and water-management techniques. From *qanat*s in Persia to flowing spring waters channelled into gardens in Kashmir, the garden became a multipurpose place. Over time, gardens were developed to great sophistication as Timur established pleasure gardens in Samarkand and named them after his conquests. In Hindustan, Babur used his palace and garden for his retreats as at Aram Bagh in Agra. The Quran suggests two sets of gardens (*Sura 55*).

Below: Produced during the Safavid period, this Kirman carpet or Wagner rug is one of the most extraordinary carpets surviving today as it depicts paradise on earth, the absolute char bagh as seen in Persia and also the concept of paradise as described in the Quran. This includes water channels which run across the garden, and a central pool. Trees, bushes, flowering plants and fruit trees are woven in with many animals, both predators and prey, as well as details such as butterflies and moths. It is one of the finest renditions of the sacred garden.

But for he who has feared the position of his Lord are two gardens. (Sura 55.46)

So which of the favours of the Lord would you deny? (Sura 55.47)

Having [spreading] branches. (Sura 55.48)

So which of the favours of your Lord would you deny? (Sura 55.49)

In both of them are two springs, flowing.[3] (Sura 55.50)

Right: The perfection of the Taj Mahal reflected in its impeccable alignment from every angle, indicates a very precise and scientific design. With each architectural feature complementing the other, the monument is flawlessly executed.

So the evolution and sophistication achieved in the *char bagh* as 'gardens of paradise' is perhaps apocryphal. That said, *jannat* was allegorically a garden and, therefore, tomb-gardens were a logical development.

The Taj Mahal, though, takes this speculation a step further as the idea of building a mausoleum as *jannat* is undoubtedly that moment of self-aggrandisement which has given us the enduring legacy of one of the world's most distinguished monuments. The building of this complex must be seen as an enormous creative and technological feat, merging science, astronomy and a vast range of skills to achieve this imagination. Shah Jahan's choice of site was not simply picturesque or defined merely by a good view from the Musamman Burj. It was conceived in perfect accordance with cosmological and cardinal alignments determining how it was to be physically inscribed on the site.

From his choice of land to the grand plan, Shah Jahan possibly had a much larger ambition than building a mere mausoleum. Central to this was the fast-flowing Yamuna, with fresh water from the melting snows of the Himalayas. *Jannat*, it is believed, would have fresh-flowing water – a pre-requisite for the creation of this other world, marking a departure from the earlier constructions of *char bagh*s. It is here that the bodies of the emperor and his wife were placed in a north-south alignment, facing west, with the possibility of their heads allegorically refreshed and replenished by the fresh-flowing water, while the feet faced south, towards the main gate and the entry for the common man who would, in Indian tradition, only salute at their feet.

The allegories are profound and require one to expand the understanding of the Taj Mahal from a symbol of love to one in which the multiple narratives and subtexts are deeply complex. The use of white marble and the metaphor of its purity also have immense implications and are yet to be fully deciphered. Certainly, the appropriation of the river in his grand plan was as stupendous an idea as the notion that he could build *jannat*. In this perception lies the possibility of exploring the reflections of the Taj Mahal, ephemeral in the flowing waters of the Yamuna and perhaps more predictably framed in the pools of Mehtab Bagh across the river.

In the Taj Mahal, multiple small and big ideas have been executed to a level of perfection. It was built long after Angkor Wat, the City of God, where too cosmology was the basis for

Following pages: The Taj Mahal is designed to be seen almost in its entirety from the riverfront. The mosque and Mehman Khana or Jawab seem to surround the mausoleum intentionally, their red sandstone serving to highlight the pristine white of the mausoleum.

its design, and the line between King and God was blurred. At the top of Angkor Wat, the celestial pools are also quartered as indeed are Sigirya's water gardens in Sri Lanka which pre-date the Taj by several centuries. The celestial pools and *char baghs* are reflections of each other, the positive and the negative – in one, water is central, and in the other, land. In each, cosmology dictated the plan, reflecting a deeply motivated desire to understand and represent the unknown, perhaps even the origins of creation.

The story of the Taj Mahal today is often that of the overwhelming magnificence of a man who loved his wife so deeply that he built this sublime monument. But the narrative is more complex – of a man consumed by passion for his wife, illusions of grandeur in wanting to make *jannat* on earth, and his desire to ensure his own immortality through this monument. Many other stories are yet to be explored – sketches

of how its design might have been etched in stone; gardens that transformed every season on the emperor's whim; water systems that nourished the landscape; fantastical flowers in perpetual mourning, and markings left behind by faceless craftspeople who made all this possible.

Standing at the podium of the Taj Mahal, looking down at the turbid waters of the Yamuna, one can hardly imagine the excitement of the Mughals who settled in Agra because of its pure snow-fed waters. But there are many evolving ideas, not least that the Yamuna was appropriated by Shah Jahan as the centrepiece of his grand design for the Taj Mahal.

Contemporarily in Europe, the Renaissance was underway and a more cultured way of life was gaining ground as castles and forts gave way to palaces of immense luxury and grandeur, starting with the Medicis in Florence in the 15th century. Elsewhere, nation-states were beginning to form and in France, Spain and Britain, a palace was a symbol of power for the monarchs of the 17th century. In France, the Louvre and Fontainebleau were converted from dismal castles into lavish palaces and similar transformations were taking place across Europe. In Hindustan, in many ways, the Taj Mahal became the symbol of the end of the Mughal Empire, while in North America, the foundation of Harvard University and several other universities were laid – a precursor to the construction of centres of learning and knowledge. St Peters in Rome and St Paul's in London were also being built, with immense domes that were symbolic of the Church's supremacy and power, distinct from those of the State. Against this backdrop of great buildings, the Taj Mahal stands apart for the rich narratives and symbolism rolled into a single complex and yet codified piece of architecture and landscape. The Taj Mahal is imagination made tangible yet evasive.

Agra's fate was also linked to its ruler. Historically at the crossroads of Indian civilisation, during Akbar's rule, it was described as the 'emporium of the traffic of the world'. The city played a pivotal role in the history of India but its own fortunes were determined when India was ruled from here. Shah Jahan moved his capital to Delhi soon after he built Shahjahanabad, and as the cost of construction of the Taj Mahal began to bankrupt the city, Agra's destiny was sealed. Once a centre of trade and great cultural traditions, with royal patronage now shifted to Delhi, the fate of the monument, and the city which flourished around

Left: The Sigirya Palace complex in Sri Lanka was built between 477 and 495 AD. Located atop a hill; at the mid level of the palace there are enormous sculptures and frescoes and at the lowest level there are elaborate water gardens. The main royal garden connects to the palace via four water channels, effectively creating a quartered garden, arguably the precursor to the char bagh. The next section consists of a path flanked by two long pools fed from nearby streams. Small ponds with man-made islands on either side of the narrow pools make an elaborate water garden complex. The plan combined concepts of symmetry and asymmetry to intentionally interlock the man-made geometrical and natural forms of the surroundings, including sophisticated surface or sub-surface hydraulic systems, some of which are still working today. The south contains a man-made reservoir to serve the complex.

Left: Angkor Wat was built later in 802-1220 AD. Symbolically, believed to be a replica of the universe in stone, representing an earthy model of the cosmic world, it's central tower symbolises the mythical Mount Meru as the centre of the universe. Some scholars believe the geographical location of the Angkor complex and the arrangement of its temples were based on sacred geography, cosmology and astronomical calculations, not unlike the Taj Mahal.

it, floundered. Behind this immense enterprise with staggering statistics, are the stories of the building of the monument and the rise and fall of the city whose destiny is inextricably linked to it. Shah Jahan lived a life of colossal excess at the cost of the people who made it possible. While there are no records of the impoverishment of the workforce at the Taj Mahal, certainly in 1632, Hindustan was in the grip of a famine, and Mughal wars further laid to waste huge tracts of land which would contribute in no small part to the decline of the Mughal Empire.

The city which sourced its life and energy from the river with its waterfront gardens, tombs, grand mansions and its prosperous trade with merchants, traders, Jesuits and mercenaries constantly pouring in, gradually dissipated once the economic hub moved north. Gone were the days when music, art and literature had flourished alongside vast tanneries engaged in making leather shoes for the Mughal armies, the mahouts who trained fighting elephants and the craftsmen who catered to the insatiable desire to build and embellish the city. Agra, once a cosmopolitan capital city, was doomed. As the Mughal power declined and marauders stripped the heart of India, even the sacred tomb was desecrated. Colonial rulers danced on the platform once used by the devout, and young lovers etched their names on the glass windows of the *hasht bihisht*. But for the common sense of Lord Curzon in the late 19th century, much more would have been lost. Clearing the gardens of overgrowth, he made valiant efforts to protect and promote the Taj Mahal. Much of how one views the Taj Mahal in present times is circumscribed by his views on neatness and order.

Today, the Taj Mahal and Agra Fort, both World Heritage Sites, still dominate the riverfront. They have attracted

Above and left: Contemporarily, in Europe, the Renaissance was underway and a more cultured way of life was gaining ground as castles and forts gave way to palaces of immense luxury and grandeur. Nation-states were beginning to form and in France, Spain and Britain, shifting from forbidding forts, the palace became a symbol of power as seen in the Tuileries and Versailles. In Hindustan, the Taj Mahal, perhaps unintentionally, became the symbol of the end of the Mughal Empire, even as Shajahanabad was being built in Delhi around the same time.

national and international concern for their protection. A Public Interest Litigation filed in 1984 sought to control industrial pollution which was threatening to discolour the white marble of the Taj Mahal. The Taj Trapezium was notified and, today, no polluting industry can operate within a 50-km radius of the monument. Moreover, in a law unprecedented in the history of preservation, a green belt of 500 metres has been provided around the Taj Mahal.

The Taj Mahal, the jewel in India's crown will be preserved for future generations. But the city has many more stories to be told – it has a successful marble craft trade, even though its tanneries were shut down by 1994, Agra remains one of the largest shoe-manufacturing centres, a legacy of Emperor Akbar who ordered shoes for his army, which were then made here. Akbar had mandated by law for the first time in Hindustan that all soldiers were required to wear shoes. Many such skilled workers including jewellers, goldsmiths, carpet weavers and marble craftsmen survive in a city which, despite repeatedly losing its economic moorings, and not least because of the Taj Mahal, still prevails. Theirs are tales of resilience and grit that form the invisible backbone of Agra's history.

New opportunities to craft a road map to bring the Taj back to its people require vision, determination and the exploration of the multiple narratives that make Agra and the Taj Mahal a potentially rich landscape and a true wonder of the world. India has the opportunity to craft its own road map to valourising its heritage but it needs vision to be inclusive of the citizens to whom these monuments belong, meshing the past and the present in imagining as well as constructing the future.

Left: The changing fortunes of Agra have impacted the economy of the city. The once-prosperous waterfront Mughal capital became a small-town industrial hub with small-scale industries causing hazardous pollution, endangering the pristine white marble of the Taj Mahal. The historic Supreme Court judgement of 1994 created the Taj Trapezium, banning all polluting industries within a 50-km radius, resulting in a major economic slump from which the city struggled to recover. Today the snow-fed waters of the River Yamuna are almost stagnant and highly contaminated.

Following pages: Dominating the waterfront and the landscape of Agra, the Taj Mahal was viewed from the boats which plied on the Yamuna, as Shah Jahan himself had visualised it.

مسال یا بگیره و فضل و سنگ انداز با بنتام مخلص حقیقت پیوند قاسم خان میرر بر و جبه به فرنگی

و فیروزی صورت و نقش اختتام گرفت

1

Building the Riverfront City

The future of Agra is inextricably linked to that of the Taj Mahal. Each time Agra struggles to surface from economic collapse, its heritage is compromised as is its position as a waterfront city. Once considered one of the noblest cities in the world and even compared with Constantinople, Agra risks being totally eclipsed in the transformations that characterise contemporary India; its rich and vibrant heritage seems to be consumed by the contingencies of survival as a city without purpose and one without a clearly defined economic trajectory. It is most difficult to visualise today its glory as a riverfront city once lined with pleasure gardens, and where the river and the mobility of people and goods on it symbolised the importance of the city and the evolving hedonistic culture that came to define the great Mughals.

Historically, cities on the Ganga and Yamuna river basins which sustained most of north India, were located on one bank of the river. The Yamuna, once an enormous river fed by the melting snows of the Himalayas in summer and the warm rains of the monsoon, doubled its size as it swept across the northern plains of India, often changing its course, flooding huge tracts of land and leaving behind rich alluvial soil. It was the most fertile river basin upon which much of north India depended and settlements along it were built judiciously, respecting the ever-shifting and uncertain course of the river.

Settlements in India were always located close to rivers as this provided access to broader networks in the region. The river basins particularly of the Ganga and Yamuna were densely populated due to the advantages of this expansive regional geography, its fertile soil and the immense network of settlements in its hinterland. This is seen as early as 500 BC in the historic city of Pataligrama

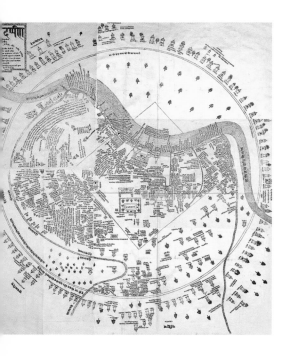

Above: Kashidarpana, the famous ancient map of Kashi accentuates its symbiotic relationship with the river – one could not exist without the other.

on the banks of the Ganga as water, cultivable lands, extensive forests and access to riverine trade were basic requirements for a sustainable settlement. As a result, the form of the city became very particular, with clear architectural responses to access the river in the form of *ghats*, as well as to celebrate its edges in the form of well-articulated walls and embankments, and then punctuating these with pavilions and other such architectural elements that signified a celebration of the river and its presence in the people's lives.

The riverfront was defined by three major fortified cities built over many centuries on the west bank of the Yamuna – Delhi, the capital city of the Sultanate; Vrindavan, with its sacred space as the birthplace of Lord Krishna, and Agra, further south, the Mughal capital of India. Between these three great cities on the Yamuna, the river swept across the Indian plains in immense oxbows. The Yamuna frequently changed its course and submerged vast tracts of lands. The stability of these cities depended on how they were built, articulating the edge of the river to ensure that it was to be momentarily trained. An entire architectural expression arose from this interface between man and water, symbolising creation, renewal and destruction or erasure.

Agra was one such city and perhaps one of the most significant early cities on the Indo-Gangetic plains, situated

Below: The seven cities of Delhi were also largely developed along the waterfront. This was primarily because access to the river ensured water supply to the settlement but also the river was a transport and trade lifeline.

Right: Calcutta was essentially dependent on river trade which came down the Ganges from the north and west. Calcutta's fortunes flourished on trade from the hinterland and its tidal river was the lifeline for its prosperity. Built on the east of the river, the city has spread north and south, while industrial development which was much later took place on its west bank.

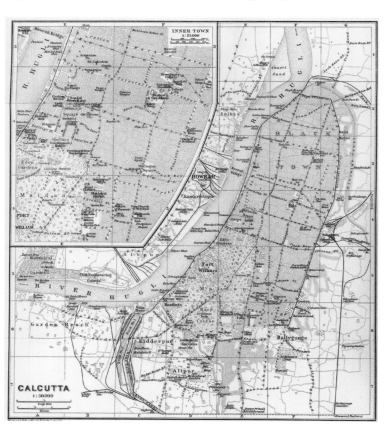

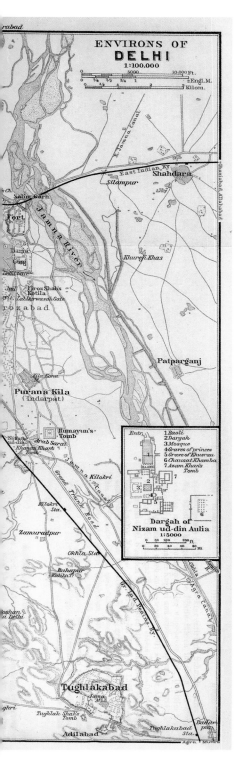

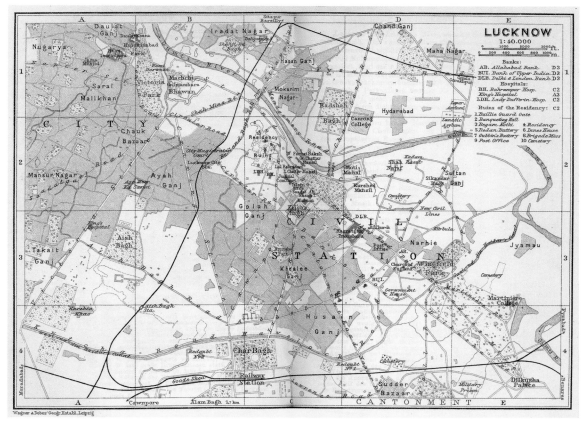

not far from the holy city of Vrindavan. It finds mention in the Mahabharata as Agravana or the forest of Agra. It is plausible that Agravana lay on the outskirts of the flourishing empire of Sursena of Mathura somewhere in 1800 BC. The first person who referred to Agra by its present name was Ptolemy 1 Soter, Alexander's trusted general and geographer, who travelled in the region in 323–283 BC. In the 10th century, Muhammad Shah, a descendent of Ghazni, invaded the city and captured it from the ruling Chauhans. The first recorded history of Agra, however, dates back to AD 1475, during the reign of Badal Singh. In 1475, Badal Singh built a brick fort known as Badalgarh as a defence against the continuous waves of Muslim invasions sweeping across the northern plains of Hindustan. It was a well-fortified city that eventually fell to the powerful and ruthless Sikander Lodi.[1]

Lodi captured Agra at the turn of the century and under his rule, the city flourished, gaining the reputation of being the Shiraz of Hindustan as Persian became the court language. Agra gained importance even though in 1505, the year Lodi moved here, it was devastated by an earthquake and had to be extensively rebuilt. Agra became known for its wealth, and the city flourished as eminent scholars, Sufi saints and poets came to the court of the Lodi Sultans. Soon, Agra became a

Above: Nestled on the banks of the Gomti, a tributary of the Ganga, Lucknow was believed to have sacred qualities as the city developed as the capital of the former princely state of Awadh. It developed as a centre of high art and culture under successive rulers over the centuries and is today at the centre of the State's heritage arc, connecting the riverfront cities of Agra and Varanasi.

47

Above: An early Mughal painting shows Babur entertaining in Sultan Ibrahim Lodi's palace, a much simpler building without much elaboration although it has a pavilion on the roof.

Facing page, far right: This painting of Babur with his courtiers from the Baburnama by Farukh Beg (c.1580-1690) indicates the emperor's love for gardens, merging them with the court.

centre of political and cultural activities. Sikander Lodi was succeeded by Ibrahim Lodi whose prosperity was short-lived as Mughal invasions began to sweep across north India.

EMPIRE OF THE MUGHALS

Agra grew to be one of the most prosperous cities in the world under the Mughals. It was occupied by Babur, the first Mughal emperor of Hindustan who ruled briefly from here. Born in 1483, Zahir-ud-din Muhammad Babur, the fifth-generation descendant of Timur, ascended the throne of Fergana at the age of 11. Although he coveted Samarkand, which he believed was his rightful inheritance, he had to settle for Kabul. Kabul, he said, was a petty province, though with enemy Uzbeks and Timurids entrenched all around and its high impassable mountains, it was relatively secure. For most of the year, Kabul was a cosmopolitan city on the trade route between Central Asia and India. 'Up from Hindustan came ten, fifteen, twenty thousand caravans bringing slaves, cotton cloth, refined sugar and spices.'[2]

From Kabul, Babur planned and executed his invasions of Hindustan, believing this was his right as Timur's most important descendant. He crossed the Indus and the five rivers of the Punjab before defeating Ibrahim Lodi at the first Battle of Panipat in 1526. The battle was one of India's most defining battles, as much for Babur as it was for Hindustan and the foundation of the Mughal Empire.

The *Baburnama* which the emperor personally dictated, remains the most evocative record of his life. For 26 years, since he captured Kabul as a young man, Babur had craved for Hindustan. Finally, 'God, through his great grace vanquished and reduced a foe like Ibrahim Sultan and made possible for us a realm like Hindustan. Hindustan...is a strange country...so many cities and so many provinces – yet there is no running water anywhere...the only running water was in the large rivers. The cities were dependent on still waters. Cities were unpleasant, houses were without walls, and people lived on monsoon-fed wells and ponds.'[3]

He records in detail India's agricultural cropping patterns linked to the monsoon rains, and spring crops which required no water and were watered by old-fashioned waterwheels or buckets. 'In Agra, Chandra and Bayana, fields were watered by means of a bucket. This is a laborious and filthy method.'[4]

Even though the heat and *andhi* of Hindustan were oppressive, Babur felt the nicer aspect was that it was 'a large country with lots of gold and money.'[5] He acknowledged 'the unlimited numbers of craftsmen and practitioners of every trade. For every labour and every product, there is an established group who have been practising that craft or professing that trade for generations... In Agra alone, there were 680 stone-masons working on my building every day.'[6]

Babur ruled Hindustan but he yearned for Kabul and was determined to create a garden of great beauty such as he enjoyed in Kabul. At Agra, he crossed the river and chose to build his first garden here. His thirst for running water was quenched by the 'snow-fed'[7] waters of the Yamuna which he describes in terms of the environment and culture of Hindustan: 'I always thought that one of the chief faults of Hindustan was that there was no running water. Everywhere that was habitable, it should be possible to construct waterwheels, create running water, and make planned geometric spaces. A few days after coming to Agra [Hijra 932... AD 1526], I crossed the Jumna with this plan in mind and scouted around for places to build a garden, but everywhere I looked was so unpleasant and desolate that I crossed back in disgust. Because the place was so ugly and disagreeable, I abandoned my dream of making a *char bagh*. Although there was no really suitable place near Agra, there was nothing to do but work with the space we had. The foundation was the large well from which the waters for the bathhouse came. Next, the patch of ground with *imbli* trees and an octagonal tank became the great pool and courtyard. Then came the pool in front of the stone building and the hall. I next finished the private garden and its outbuildings, and after that, I completed the bathhouse. Thus in unpleasant and inharmonious India, marvellously regular and geometric gardens were introduced. In every corner, there are beautiful plots and every plot was laid out with roses and narcissus. We suffered three things in Hindustan. One was the heat, another, the biting wind, and the third, dust. The bathhouse was a refuge from all three. The bathhouse has no dust or wind and in the hot weather, it is so cool that one almost feels the chill. One chamber of the bath, the one with the warm water reservoir, was finished in stone. The *dado* was of white stone; otherwise the floor and ceiling were of red stone from Bayana. Khalifa, Shaykh Zayn, Yunus Ali and all who acquired lands along the river, built geometric and beautifully planned gardens and ponds. As is done in Lahore and Dipalpur, they made running water with waterwheels. The men of Hind who had never before seen places form on such a plan, or laid out

49

Right: In a garden in bloom, Babur seated on his throne, meets his courtiers and receives a written document. In front of him is the central pool of the char bagh with ducks, and trees with birds, all artfully painted.

Above: Jahangir is entertained by Nur Jahan in a pavilion in a char bagh. *The painting shows how much the Mughal emperors enjoyed gardens. Jahangir was a prolific builder of garden complexes in Agra where he built the Jahangir pavilion at Aram Bagh and then gifted the garden to Nur Jahan as her* jagir. *His most significant gardens were in Kashmir.*

Above: Painted in 1590, Babur is shown seated on a low platform beneath a scarlet rectangular canopy, receiving Uzbek envoys in a garden full of flowers and blossoming trees. Behind him are the red sandstone walls of a city, with a small doorway, indicating how visitors had to enter the fortified city.

Bottom: Aram Bagh which in its time would have been redolent with flowers and fruit was an immense undertaking as pathways and water channels intersect across the entire garden, and was built by Babur during his very brief reign.

Facing Page above and centre: The waterfront walls were always defined by burjs which seem to anchor the walls but also had wells, lifts and water systems within, which fed the entire garden complex.

Below: Later additions by Emperor Jahangir included pleasure pavilions along the waterfront.

with so much elegance, gave the name of Kabul to the side of the Jumna on which these structures stood.'[8]

There is no clarity as to which was actually the first garden so described, or indeed if Aram Bagh was the first place where Babur spent time establishing his gardens and baths, in effect a palace-garden. It was where he could command order in a disorderly land, and make the transition from chaos, heat and dust to a secluded space with fruit, flowers, water and private pleasure chambers of *hammam*s and *tehkhana*s. Water in arid lands was as much a lifeline as high walls ensured total privacy. Effectively, in Hindustan as much as in Kabul or Samarkand, pleasures of nobility could be enjoyed to the hilt in absolute seclusion. The emperor had constructed what he had imagined as a paradise garden – internalised and exclusive.

Babur developed gardens in the classical sense of a walled *char bagh* but introduced many innovations used in other gardens in Hindustan. The raised platform along the river's edge was ideal as a terrace along the waterfront and ingeniously served to raise water from the river; it was from this terrace that water was distributed to the garden. The *hammam*s were built under the high waterfront terrace, with several chambers including a beautifully painted main chamber, all of which were fed by a network of channels. In summer, this cloistered space would

have been cool and it is said that Babur conducted his business from here. In winter, an elaborate heating system ensured hot baths to maintain the lifestyle, offering both pleasure and refuge.

Water was drawn from the river by a series of Persian waterwheels, and would also flow into the network of canals and tanks which divided the *char bagh*. Babur modelled his garden on those he saw in Kabul, with descending terraces and cascading water which pleased the senses but were, above all, practical. Since the area was largely flat, the feature of water cascades was possible because of the raised terrace. The water was then transported in channels through the *char bagh*, providing pleasure pools and cascades as well as irrigation systems which sustained the garden. These were graduated to descend towards the far end of the garden.

As in Central Asia, a high garden wall provided protection from the elements, and privacy for the users. At the far end of the immense garden leading into the settlements, the *bagh* had an impressive gateway with a massive studded wooden door befitting an emperor. The emperor and his nobles arrived by barge and entered from the riverside pier, while the far gateway was used by the laity. The scale of the entrance was indicative of the royal domain.

The lives of the Mughals alternated between long hard years in the battlefield and extreme luxury, and Babur's refuge was Gul Afshan. His lasting legacy in Hindustan was Mughal gardens, replicated over generations across Hindustan in fort and palace architecture.

His grandson Jahangir especially shared his ancestor's love of flora and fauna and invested in fragrant flower gardens. Between 1615 and 1619, he built two pleasure pavilions on the riverfront terrace in Agra, with decorative paintings and a large tank with fountains and a platform which would have lent itself to Jahangir's lifestyle. 'On this day, I went to see the Garden of Gul Afshan which is on the banks of the Jumna. On the way, rain fell heavily and filled the mead with freshness and greenness. Pineapples had arrived at perfection and I made a thorough inspection. Of the buildings that overlook

The building of riverfront gardens was an engineering feat. High walls banked the waterfront and a highly sophisticated water-lifting system, introduced by Babur at Aram Bagh (right), first served the hammams, then the garden. This system was then used in other riverfront gardens (top, above, top, centre) which drew water from the river and then distributed it throughout the gardens. Over time, the water-lifting system became more elaborate.

54

the river, none that I saw were without the charm of verdure and flowing water.'[9]

Jahangir loved this pleasure garden, second only to his beloved Kashmir, and frequently stayed here, renaming it Bagh-I-Nur Afshan, giving it as a part of Nur Jahan's *jagir*. 'On Wednesday, together with the ladies seated in a boat, I went to Nur Afshan and rested there at night. As the garden belongs to the establishment of Nur Jahan B., on Thursday 4th, she held the royal entertainment and presented great offering.'[10]

In the summer of 1530, Humayun was taken seriously ill and in one of the most famous recorded incidents of his life, Babur is said to have carried out a ritual in which he offered his own life to save his son's. As it turned out, Humayun recovered, but Babur's health deteriorated, and in December 1530, he died in Agra. He was first buried in a nearby garden,

Below: In time, the riverfront was defined by high walls and burjs, often edge-to-edge. Riverfront mansions and gardens were owned by princes, princesses and nobility who received these lands as jagirs. The lush gardens filled with fruit and flower, sparkling water channels and ponds were accessible only by a chosen few. The contrast between verdant gardens in a secluded environment and the city bustling with traders, merchants, bazaars, serais and havelis was undoubtedly stark.

and later, between 1539 and 1544, taken to his beloved Kabul. Babur's original burial site, Chauburj, is a dismal reminder of better days. A few square feet of grass surrounded by a low wall are all that remain of it.

In Agra, Babur built the first *char bagh*. It is widely believed that Aram Bagh was the first complete *char bagh* in Hindustan. Noted historian, Ebba Koch, in her book, *The Complete Taj Mahal*, proposes that Babur's first garden in Agra was Chahar Bagh or Bagh-i-Hasht Bihisht, situated almost opposite the Taj Mahal. There are no traces of the garden today. In his last year though, Babur does note that he was returning to his *hasht bihisht* in Agra.

Mughal garden scholar Sylvia Crowe is of the view that Aram Bagh is the original garden, as Zahara Bagh which was built for his daughter, is alongside Aram Bagh. Today, a highway has erased Zahara Bagh and even torn into the aqueducts of Aram Bagh, believed to have been renamed Ram Bagh by the Marathas in the 18th century. Historian R. Nath believes that Babur commanded buildings to be put up in Agra on the other side of the river, and a stone palace to be built for himself between the *haram* and the garden. He also had one built in the audience court, with a reservoir in the middle and four chambers in the four towers. On the river's bank, he had a *chaukandi* built.

Following Babur's death, Humayun struggled for years to secure his father's legacy. Babur, in the tradition of his forefathers Timur and Genghis Khan, had ensured each of his sons inherited a piece of Hindustan to consolidate and rule as best as they could, but Humayun lacked Babur's drive for power and possession at a time when it was the only currency for survival. He was unable to consolidate his father's conquests and spent over 15 years in exile while he rebuilt his army and his relationship with Shah Tahmasp of Persia before he could return to reclaim Hindustan.

In the interim, Hindustan was ruled by Sher Shah Suri and it was only after the death of his son which left the kingdom weak and untended, that Humayun was empowered enough to return to Delhi and his fort, Dinpannah, for a very brief period before famously slipping to his death on his library stairs.

Akbar, grandson of Babur was merely 13 years old when he became Hindustan's youngest Mughal emperor in 1555. Jalal-ud-din Muhammad Akbar, contemporaneous with Shakespeare would, like Shakespeare, die on his birthday at the age of 63. One of India's greatest emperors, Akbar conquered

Above: This portrait of Akbar in his old age, dated c. 1645, was probably commissioned by Shah Jahan, his grandson, who was just 13 when the emperor died. Mughal imperial conventions such as the golden halo and the emperor standing on an orb representing the world were developed in the court to signify Akbar's stature and power as a Mughal emperor.

Facing page: This painting from the Akbarnama, the official history of Akbar's reign, shows his mother, Mariam Makani, travelling to Agra by river. Several other boats, including that of the emperor, can be seen as well. The pomp and ceremony of the imperial boat cavalcade had to reflect the stature of an emperor.

وریاض امال ارباب اخلاص نظارت یافت و جراحت یافتکان روزگار را مرہم

شایسته پدید آمد

and united Hindustan, laying the foundations for the country as we know it today. He made Agra his capital, recognising its potential as the heart of the Mughal Empire, and set about rebuilding Agra Fort.

In the extravagant traditions of the Persian Court, his life is chronicled meticulously by Abul Fazl which he himself described as 'a pen perfumed with sincerity'[11]. Abul Fazl's *Akbarnama* and *Ain-e-Akbari* remain the most detailed accounts of the emperor to whom he remained a devoted chronicler. The description of Akbar's birth set the tone for future court recordings. 'The pains of travail came upon Her Majesty and in that auspicious moment, the unique pearl of the vice-regency came forth in his glory.'[12]

At its peak, Akbar's empire extended from Kabul to the Bay of Bengal and fell just short of the Deccan. He had conquered the richest and most prosperous kingdom with a population of all of Europe. An astute ruler, he made a shrewd assessment of the challenges ahead. Matrimonial alliances had much to do with securing peace in the neighbourhood and his endless need for soldiers. Akbar's harem, at its peak in thousands, was a multicultural undertaking. At 19, in a strategic alliance which brokered peace in Rajputana and would also influence the culture of the Mughal court, Akbar married Jodha Bai, the daughter of the Raja of Amber, and renamed her Maryam uz Zamani. Later, he married other Rajput noble women, thus securing Rajput loyalty as well as their armies. A visionary, he permitted his wives to practise Hinduism in the *zenana* and retain their traditional customs. As much as this was practical, it also exercised immense influence on the architectural styles of Mughal Agra.

The birth of his son and the building of Fatehpur Sikri, his new capital city outside Agra, also coincided with his military victories in Gujarat. He brought Gujarati artisans to work at Sikri, and in the creation of Fatehpur Sikri, he established the paradigm for what we now know as a synthesis of Hindu and Muslim architecture and design, with its rich architectural vocabulary still unparalleled in scale or ambition. Fatehpur Sikri was a brief meteoric phase in the emperor's life, and it was soon abandoned as it fell short of water and was not easily accessible. In real terms, the court never left Agra as the imperial treasuries remained at the fort simply because the fort was on the imperial highway and Sikri was not.

Akbar ruled Hindustan from Agra and Lahore, two very strategically placed capitals from where he could control his

Facing page: A later portrait of Humayun (left) and Akbar (right) showing them together, is somewhat anachronic as Akbar was merely 13 when Humayun died. Despite his young years, Akbar was already leading his armies and was in the battlefield in Kalanur when Humayun died. Bairam Khan, Humayun's trusted general, crowned Akbar the new emperor and escorted him back to Delhi.

Below: Maharaja Gaj Singh of Marwar (left) and Maharaja Jai Singh of Amber (right) c. 1630. Over time these Rajput houses would marry their daughters to Mughal emperors, achieving peace within their kingdoms as well as providing armies for the endless Mughal wars. The cultural fusion as a result of these alliances is a significant legacy of the Mughals.

Below: Chauburj, where Babur was initially buried is located fairly close to Aram Bagh. Even though his remains were moved to Kabul, Chauburj still retained its importance.

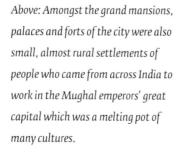

Above: Amongst the grand mansions, palaces and forts of the city were also small, almost rural settlements of people who came from across India to work in the Mughal emperors' great capital which was a melting pot of many cultures.

vast and still unruly empire. Ralph Fitch, an early British traveller observed: 'Agra is a very great citie and populous, built with stone, having faire and large streetes, with a faire river running by it, which falleth into the Gulfe of Bengala.' He further describes the two capitals: '[They]…are two very great cities. Either of them much greater than London and very populous.'[13]

With a population of around 7,50,000, Agra flourished under Akbar. Abul Fazl records his first impressions of the city: 'The River Yamuna, which has few like it for digestibility of water, flows through it. […] Agra is a large city and possesses a healthy climate. The River Yamuna flows through it for five *kos* and on either bank are delightful villas and pleasant stretches of meadow. It is filled with people from all countries and is the emporium of the traffic of the world. His Majesty has built a fort of red stone, and like of which travellers have never recorded. It contains more than five hundred buildings of masonry after the beautiful designs of Bengal and Gujarat which masterly sculptors and cunning artists of form have fashioned as architectural models…his present Majesty embellished it and thus a matchless city has arisen.'[14] Badaoni and Nizamuddin, two other contemporary historians of Akbar's time, confirm the grandeur of the city and its lofty fort.

As Agra expanded, new drainage was installed to cater to its growing population. Afghan, Uzbek, Persian merchants were among those who came to trade, so *caravanserai*s sprung up around the Fort as did tented cities to accommodate soldiers accustomed to the mobility of their calling. Leather workers

Left: Agra grew to be a significant city under Akbar, with elegant mansions or havelis, several storeys high flanking wide roads. Although the façades facing the roads were relatively simple, the havelis within had a number of courtyards, shaded gardens and housed a large number of family members and staff, its scale depending on the wealth and status of the owner.

Left and far left: The city had a protective wall around it and at night, its many gates were closed with no one permitted to enter or leave the city. These varied in scale and design. Nonetheless, they were formidable gateways.

Below: Agra flourished under Akbar, with a population of around 7,50,000. Abul Fazl records his first impressions of the city: "The River Yamuna which has few like it for digestibility of water flows through it."

On one side was the bustling city with great palaces and mansions on the waterfront, and on the other bank were pleasure gardens. It was at the time a very unique city plan.

Facing page: One of the earliest maps of Agra city and the suburbs (1850, National Archives) shows how the city had expanded way beyond the domain of grand mansions and sepulchral gardens. Even though the capital had moved to Delhi and the economy had declined after the 17th century, the city was still a significant entity when it was first mapped.

arrived at Akbar's behest to make shoes for his armies whose battles seemed unending. Clothiers, textile merchants, jewellers served the needs of the court while great *mandis* catered for this mammoth and somewhat fluid population, and provided immense supplies for royal armies, hundreds of elephants, horses, builders, gardeners, craftsmen and artisans – this was a huge enterprise which flourished under Akbar's patronage.

The city grew intensely. Communities from across the country often stayed in the same area for purposes of familiarity and succour. Areas often denoted the trade and they still do today; others are more linked to those who came and settled. Gokulpura, Baluchpura or Jaisinghpura were areas of affluence, while other areas were named after the traders or *serais*, such as Roshan Mohalla or Seth Gali. The *saib bazaar* or *loha mandi*, *kinari bazaar* or even *namak ki mandi* of today are reminders of the trade which flourished then.

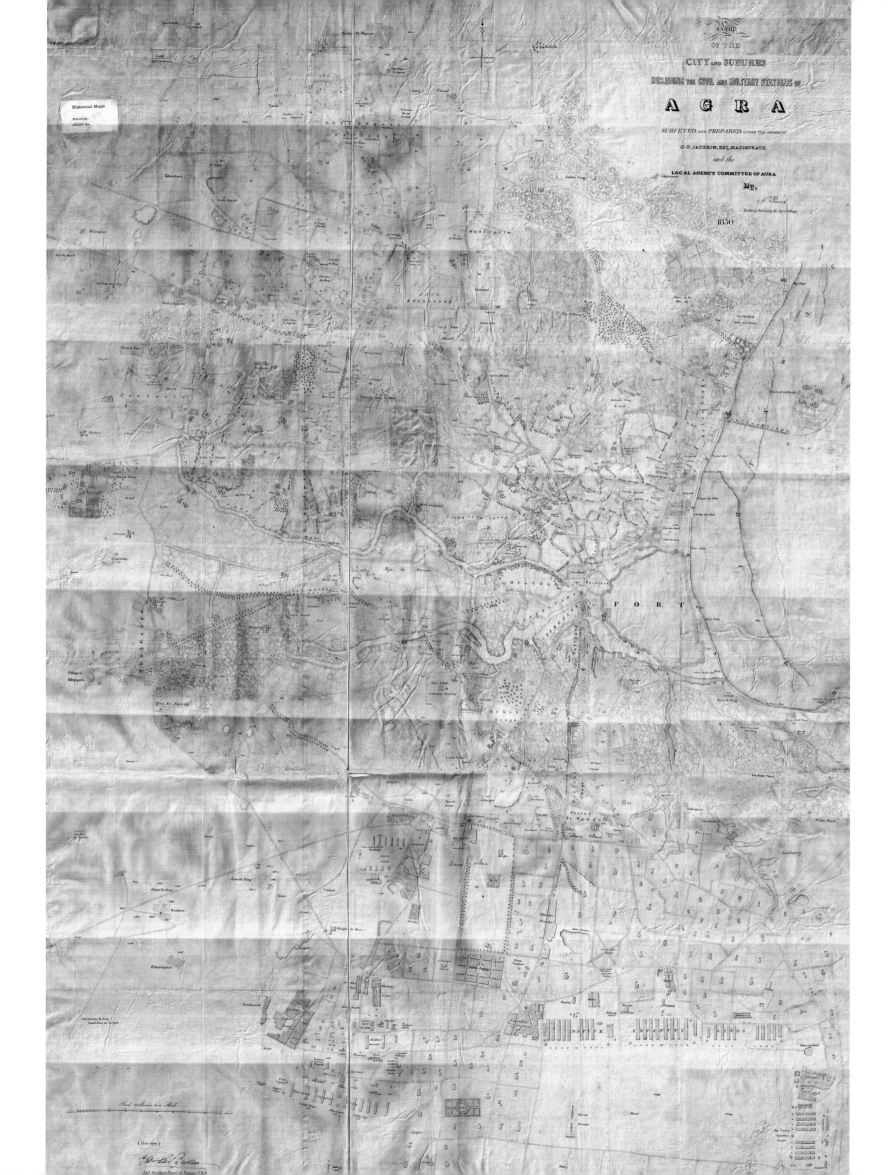

MAP
OF THE
CITY AND SUBURBS
INCLUDING THE CIVIL AND MILITARY STATIONS OF
AGRA
SURVEYED AND PREPARED UNDER THE ORDERS OF
C. O. JACKSON, ESQ. MAGISTRATE,
and the
LOCAL AGENCY COMMITTEE OF AGRA
By,

1850

FORT

The Yamuna flowed fast and was a lifeline for irrigation and transport. Its pure waters, sacred to the Hindus, made a busy waterway for Mughal barges. As in Sikander Lodi's time, royal movement as far as possible, was by barge along the river. Traders and merchants too came by boat as this was a secure royal zone where they were less likely to encounter thieves who marched the countryside.

At the entry point to Agra before Aram Bagh was a toll gate named Batees Khamba. Certainly it was at Batees Khamba that the Mughals extracted the heavy toll which underwrote the city's expenses, where general traders halted, and were often not even permitted to enter the city. If the riverfront

Facing page and below: Batees Khamba is an immense structure towering over the entry to Agra on the river edge. It was built essentially as a toll gate to control entry into Agra and extract toll which financed the Mughal coffers. Behind is the Nur Jahan serai where travellers could stay while waiting to enter the city. This was the complex which once controlled the fortunes of the city.

was flanked on both sides by palaces and pleasure gardens, Batees Khamba was where 'outsiders' were stopped, with only a select few permitted to go beyond and into the city. For those who weren't grand enough to mingle in the densely populated city, there was a *serai* which could house as many as 3000 travellers and 500 horses from where Nur Jahan also collected taxes, undoubtedly contributing to the imperial coffers.

As word about the power of the Great Mughal spread, visitors from around the world came to Akbar's court. Agra, with Agra Fort as its centre, became a cosmopolitan city.

Father Monserrate whose records of Akbar's court are well known, described the fort thus: '...he included in the confines of the citadel the mansions of his nobles, the magazines, the treasury, the arsenal, the stables of the cavalry, and the shops and huts of drug sellers, barbers and all sorts of common workmen. The stones of these buildings are so cunningly fitted that the joints are scarcely visible, although no lime was used to fix them together. The beautiful colour of the stone which is all red also produces the same effect of uniform solidity... If all had happened as he wished, Agara would have formed a fitting memorial of the king's wisdom. For, it has the advantage over almost all other cities of that region in respect of its mild climate, of its fertile soil, of its great river, of its beautiful gardens, of its fame spread to the end of the earth, and of its large size. For it is four miles long and two broad. All the necessities of human life can be obtained here if desired. This is even true of articles which have to be imported from distant corners of Europe. There are a great number of artisans, ironworkers and goldsmiths. Gems and pearls abound in large numbers. Gold and silver are plentiful, as also are horses from Persia and Tartary. Indeed the city is flooded with vast quantities of every type of commodity. Hence Agara is seldom visited by a dearth of food supplies. In addition to this, its central position (for it is, as it were, the navel of

Above and right: Agra Fort was not built in a single generation. It was first rebuilt by Akbar and subsequently embellished by Shah Jahan, his grandson, who introduced the use of white marble in the palace and court buildings. The highly detailed carving and design is the emperor's enduring legacy in both scale and refinement.

White marble palaces and imperial rooms were largely oriented to the waterfront and dominated the fort skyline, its golden domed pavilions visible across the city. Notably all the outer buildings remained in red sandstone, perhaps setting the tone for the architectural vocabulary used later in the Taj Mahal.

the whole kingdom) enabled the king whenever he had the occasion, easily to go himself in any direction, or to summon his subjects to meet him.'[15]

Agra Fort is distinctive for its massive protective wall dressed in red sandstone, some 70-feet high and 1½ miles in circumference. Encircled by a moat and along the river with direct access to the water, the fort stands high above the city, its ramparts defining the skyline, its eminence reinforced with each generation making new additions to its already elegant architecture. It is perhaps one of the most rebuilt forts in India. And although Agra Fort was already a Mughal fort, Akbar set about a massive reconstruction at a scale befitting his empire. Situated at the heart of Akbar's huge empire, it was built at a cost of three-and-a-half-million rupees, a staggering amount in those days, and took a mere eight years to complete. Although only a few structures remain of the 500 buildings in the wonderful designs of Bengal and Gujarat recorded by Abul Fazl, the fort's architectural history spans three generations of Mughal emperors.

Although rebuilt by Akbar in 1556, construction within Agra Fort continued well into the second half of the 17th century, and the reign of Aurangzeb, arguably the last great Mughal. Jahangir and Shah Jahan also contributed to the grandeur of this fort.

The impressive architectural styles of this complex are a rare amalgamation of the aesthetic sensibilities of three different Mughal emperors greatly influenced by the design aesthetic of the lands they had conquered. Shah Jahan's architectural style changed the palaces from the forbidding red sandstone structures of Akbar's reign, to delicate finely carved and inlaid marble, creating richly embellished palaces and mosques, often with material sourced from great distances. By now, Mughal architects were familiar with the vast skills available in India and presided over the emerging Mughal architectural vocabulary. The transition from Akbar's bold red sandstone as a statement of power to the refined elegance of Shahjahani white marble marked the emergence of the spiritual and temporal symbolism in Mughal architecture.

Designed for protection with double ramparts, slits and loopholes, the battlements were substantial. On the landward side, there was an additional moat with a drawbridge leading to the Delhi Gate. This is heavily decorated with a *gajyavala*. One of the most notable examples of syncretism, symbolising the indestructible power of the empire, the panel shows

Facing page: This rare painting of the Agra Fort, in the Company School style, was made by Indian artists for the British employees of the East India Company. This painting shows the fort before it was destroyed in the 1857 uprising. The massive scale of the fort is clearly visible as also its layers of buildings, from the outer public buildings to the more private palaces perched over the river. The painting also provides a clear view of the riverfront gardens across the river from the fort.

Below and bottom: The scale of the outer fortifications with a huge moat was daunting to most. Rising to great heights, with a double fortification wall on the city side, the fort was designed to be virtually impregnable.

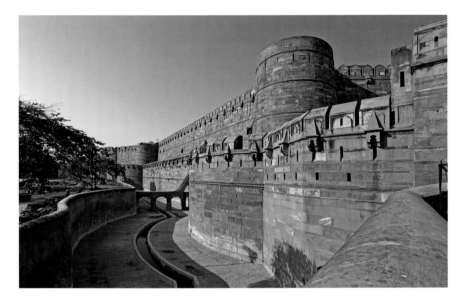

Right, far right and below: Shah Jahan's contribution to the Agra Fort is significant. He rebuilt the royal buildings, creating an immediate distinction between the royal and the secular chambers, shifting from Akbar's stately red to white marble, the change marking the merging of the spiritual and the temporal.

elephants overcome by a hybrid winged beast, reminiscent of the Assyrian griffin but comparable to the monsters of Hindu iconography, with the neck and ears of a horse, the legs and tail of a lion, the tusks and trunk of an elephant.

The magnificent Hathi Pol provides a second entry. Originally, it was flanked by two huge sandstone elephants which were destroyed by Aurangzeb who erased as much of Hindu culture as he could.

The Akbari Gate was renamed Amar Singh Gate during Shah Jahan's era and is guarded by two barbicans. A massive structure with galleries built in tiers, it provides a sense of scale much larger than it actually is.

On the waterfront lies the Khizri Gate which opened onto a pier and *ghat*s, all of which have been lost over time as the river changed its course.

Inside, the fort was organised as a city of grand scale, its many buildings flanking well laid-out streets in an established hierarchy, with the royal family quarters secluded beyond the residences of nobility, with the lesser court officials and army on the periphery.

From the ramparts of the fort, Akbar could view his famous elephant fights on a flat strip of land between the fort wall and the river. Elephant fighting was one of Akbar's favourite sports. It is said he had more than 6,000 elephants in the stable, of which 101 were his personal ones. Five men were assigned to each elephant, so this section of the fort alone would have been substantially populated.

Shah Jahan rebuilt the Diwan-e-Khas with such precision that his nobles, rather than approaching the *takht* from the front, could approach it from any angle – the alignment of the pillars was such that they could have an uninterrupted view of the *takht*. The raised platform had at its centre the legendary Takht-e-Taus or Peacock Throne commissioned by him. The ultimate symbol of ostentation, it was inlaid with precious and semi-precious stones including the Kohinoor or Babur's diamond.

The Peacock Throne's wealth was legendary and it was much coveted. Completed in the course of seven years at a cost of ten million rupees, it had 11 recesses around it for cushions, richly embellished with jewels set in 50 kilos of gold. In 1655, Tavernier, the French traveller at Shah Jahan's court described the Peacock Throne as 'a rectangular throne, six-feet long and four-feet wide and resembled a field bed. It had four sturdy legs about twenty-five inches in height and an arched canopy

BAR

DILHI GAT

FRONT

SCALE

ICAN

AGRA FORT

EVATION

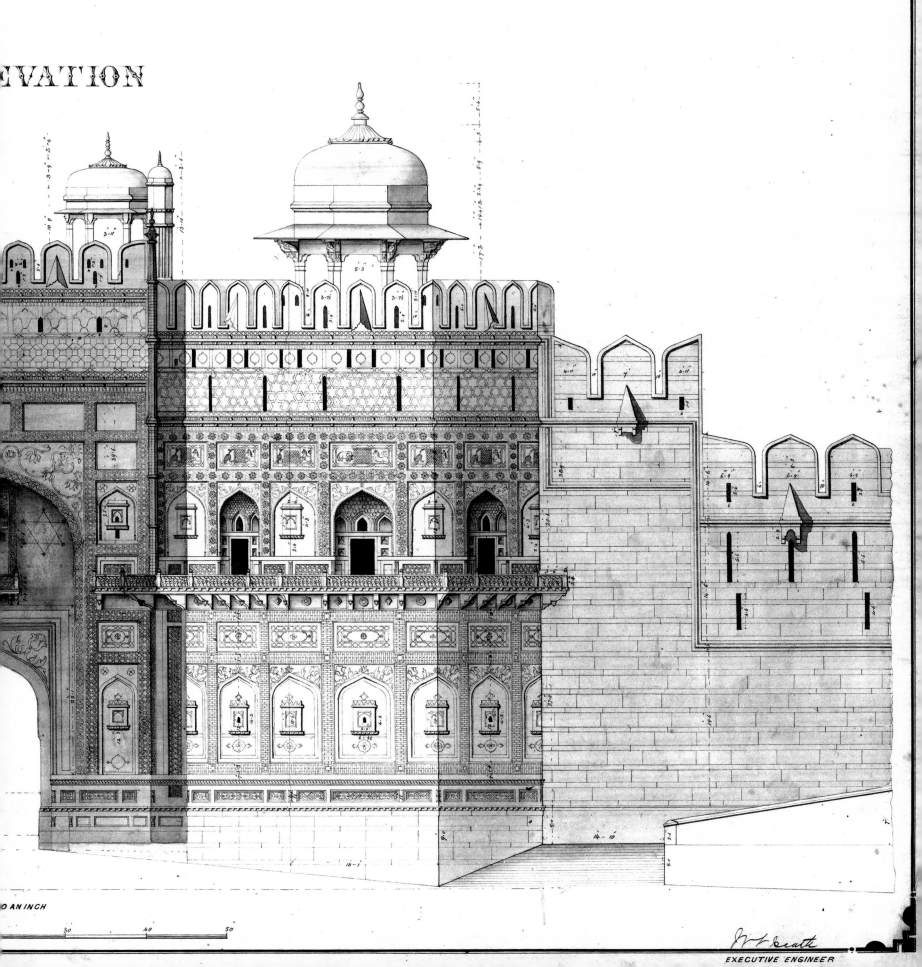

EXECUTIVE ENGINEER

DIWAN-I-KHAS, AGRA FORT

DETAIL OF CARVED FLOOR SCREEN IN WHITE MARBLE

supported by twelve columns…one peacock with an elevated tail of blue sapphires and other coloured stones, the body of gold inlaid with precious stones, having a large ruby in front of the breast whence hangs a pear-shaped pearl of about 50 carats or thereabouts.'[16]

Behind the *takht* of the emperor is a pavilion with a delicately carved screen for the women to view court proceedings. Khas Mahal is a richly decorated pavilion with fine inlay work in precious stones, with a terrace and a screen wall at the rear, overlooking the river. This was the emperor's personal chamber with three pavilions on the riverside and a fountain courtyard. The central pavilion with cusped arches, used by the emperor is a fine example of the blend of Persian and Indian design and decorative art. The two pavilions on either side have a *bangla*-style roof with gilded domes for the ladies, and wonderful little niches so narrow that only a woman's hand could reach inside to hide her jewels. The pavilions overlook Angoori Bagh, so known for the profusion of carvings of grapes.

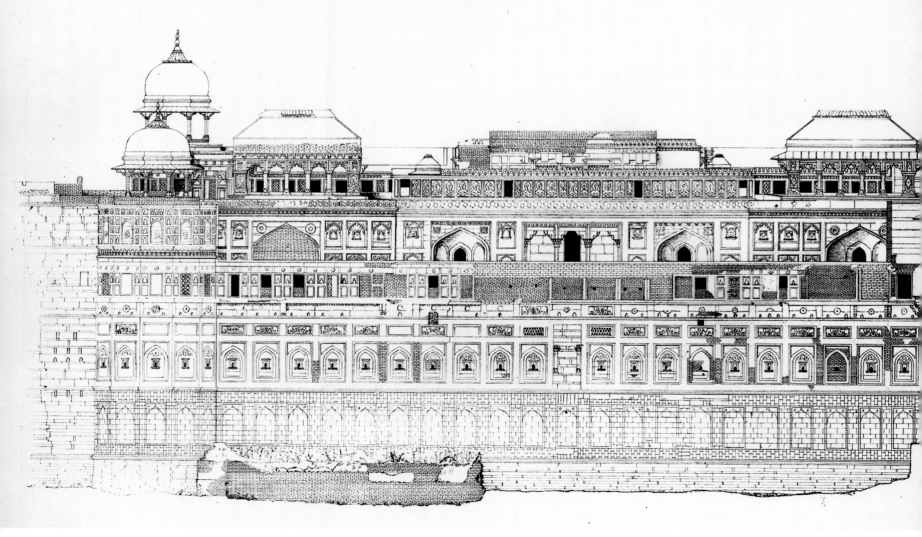

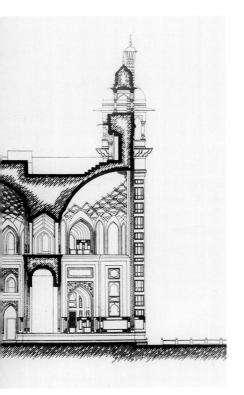

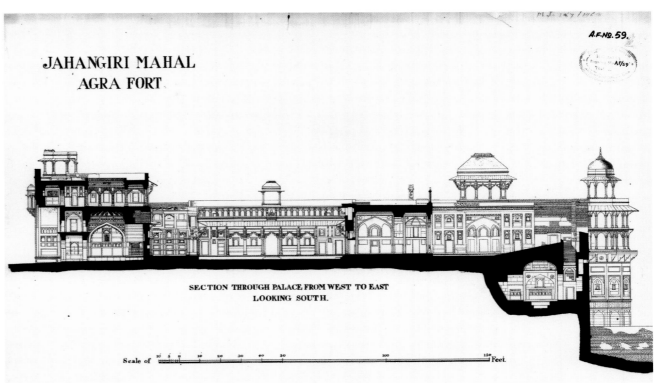

JAHANGIRI MAHAL
AGRA FORT

SECTION THROUGH PALACE FROM WEST TO EAST
LOOKING SOUTH.

Scale of Feet

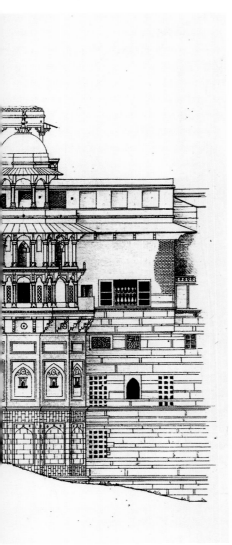

Angoori Bagh, a *char bagh* in the classic sense, is believed to have been inspired by the gardens of Kashmir. Of note also is the Macchi Bhavan, a pleasure garden with fountains and pools full of fish designed for the amusement of the harem.

Alongside is the Sheesh Mahal. With its two large halls completely covered with mica mosaic embedded in lime, it is one of the most finely crafted Mughal palaces. When the room is lit with candles, the curvature of the ceiling ensures it comes alive with myriad lights. It has ponds and channels of water running through it connecting to the *hammams* and the Musamman Burj.

Built by Shah Jahan in marble, the Musamman Burj is an octagonal tower with an open pavilion extending over the fortifications. At its centre is a stylised lotus tank with a central fountain, flamboyantly carved and inlaid with semi-precious stones. The vaulted marble roof of the pavilion was once painted with gold. The most exquisitely carved marble screen in what appears to be double layers encloses the entire area. It was in this complex that Shah Jahan spent his last days, imprisoned by his son, cared for by his daughter, viewing his beloved Taj Mahal.

The construction of mosques alongside imperial palaces and military establishments was perceived as essential to maintain the balance of power. The Moti Masjid is in the centre of the fort beyond the Diwan-e-Aam, its dome dominating the

Elaborate drawings, sections and elevations show clearly how complex the construction system was and the massive scale of the buildings which were built in a relatively short time.

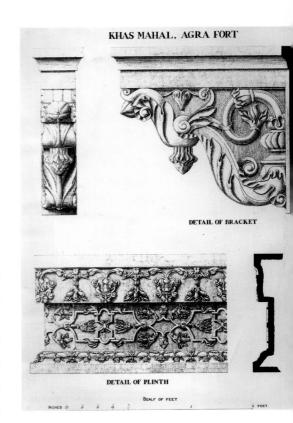

KHAS MAHAL. AGRA FORT

DETAIL OF BRACKET

DETAIL OF PLINTH

SCALE OF FEET

skyline of the Red Fort. The Nagina Masjid is a private mosque built by Shah Jahan for the ladies of the court, and the delicate Mina Masjid was built for Shah Jahan by Aurangzeb.

When Akbar died in 1605, he was succeeded by Jahangir who shifted his court to Lahore, and often stayed in Kashmir where he built exotic pleasure gardens. Jahangir was the beneficiary of Akbar's successes, and presided over an empire largely at peace. Compared to the endless campaigns which consumed Akbar, Jahangir's era was one of relative ease and he could devote himself to life's pleasures. Though he claimed Agra Fort and developed the riverfront gardens, Agra's significance was at its zenith under his son, Shah Jahan.

During Jahangir's reign, Agra was an established city with elegant mansions several storeys high, with courtyards in the centre and several *char bagh*s. The façades of the buildings that housed a vast number of family and staff, were relatively

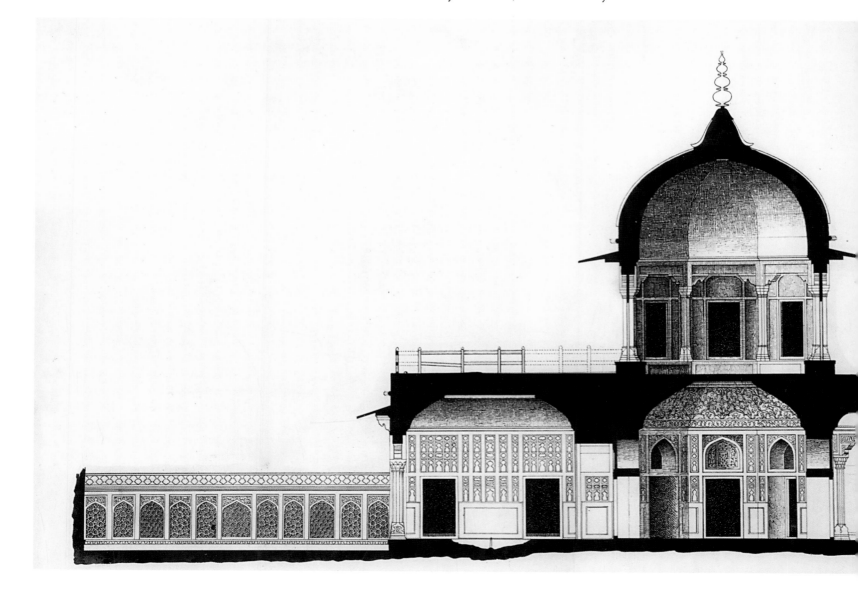

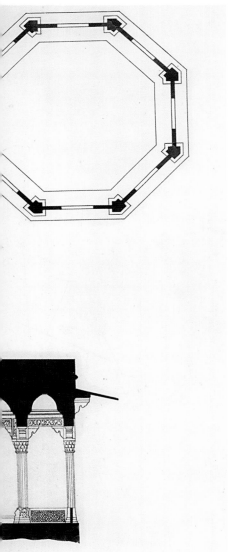

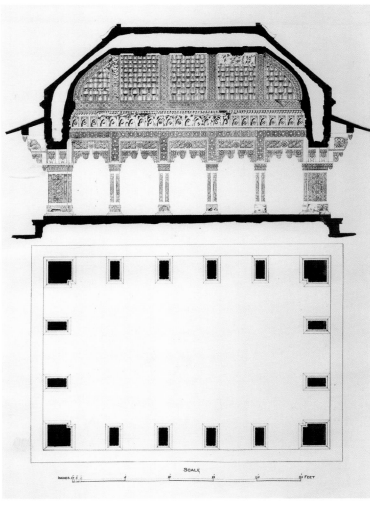

Following pages: This painting of the entire fort complex depicts its life at several levels. At the bottom, just outside the fort, an elephant fight, a favourite sport of the emperors, is underway. Shah Jahan would have watched from the marble jharokha above the fort walls. To the right, the palaces are detailed with awnings, and open courtyards are in use. Beyond is the Moti Masjid, the emperor's private mosque. Inside the complex is a camel brigade, perhaps sent by one of the Rajput rulers whose daughters had married one of the Mughals. All round on the bastions, soldiers can be seen securing the emperor's capital.
At the top, just outside the main gate, an army with foot soldiers and elephants, is probably returning from or preparing for war.

77

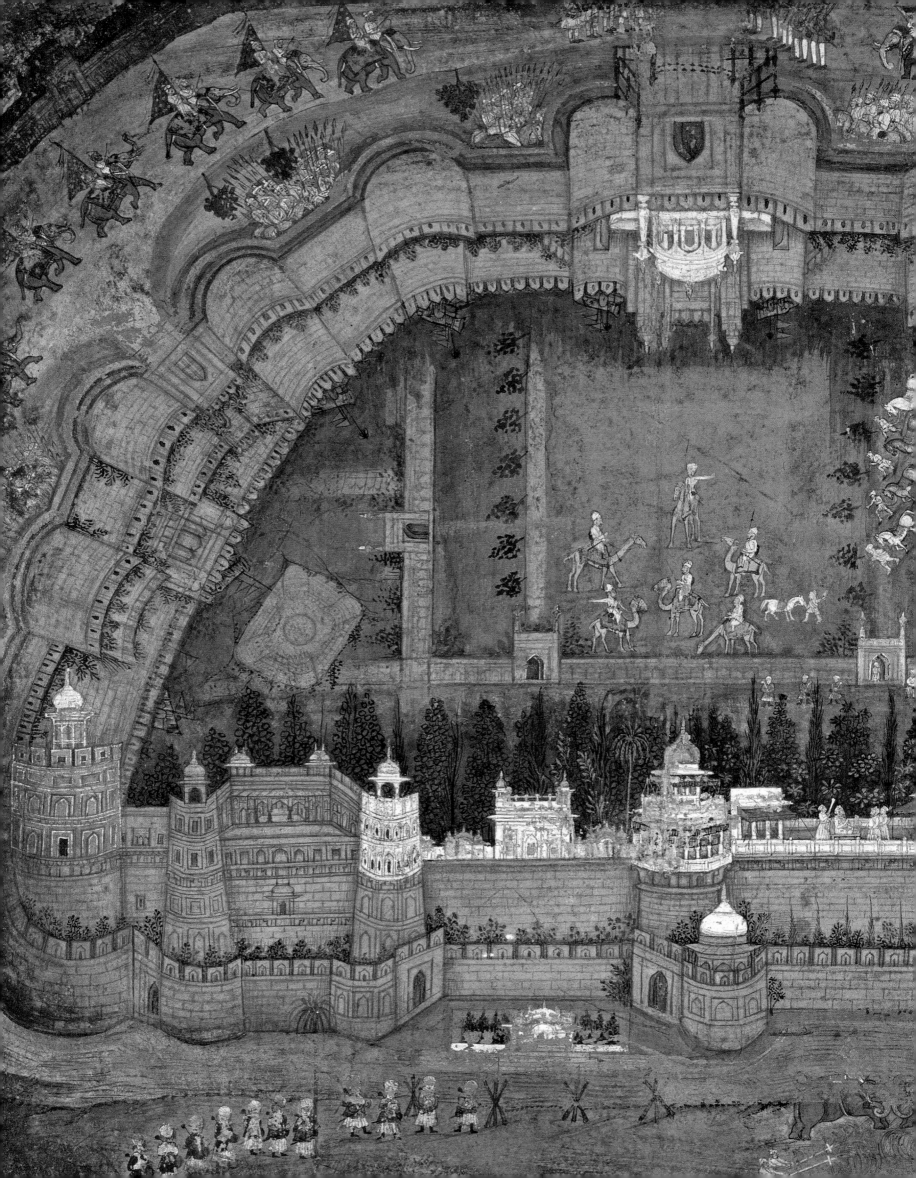

simple. Larger homes had stables for horses or even elephants. The grand mansions of Agra – homes of nobility and wealthy merchants – were built on the east bank of the river opposite the pleasure gardens. John Jourdain, an East India Company employee visiting the city in 1610 wrote in his journal that the city was by repute 'far greater than Cairo... There is a great resort of people to that city from all parts of the world that you cannot desire anything but you shall find it in this city. It is very populous, insomuch that when you ride along in the streets, you must have a man or two to go before to thrust aside the people, for they are so thick as in a fair in our country... This city is of great trade from all places. Here you may find merchants that will pass money to all places of the Indias, Persia and Aleppo.'[17]

William Finch, an indigo trader, visited Agra in 1610 and in his valuable records of the city, says that Agra '...is spacious, large, populous beyond measure, that you can hardly passé in the streets, which are for the most part dirty and narrow, save only the great bazaar and some few others, which are large and faire. The citie lyeth in manner of a halfe-moon, bellying to the land-ward some 5 c. (kos) in length and as much by the riverside, upon the bankes whereof are many goodly houses of nobility, pleasantly over-looking Gemini, which runneth with a swift current from the north to the south somewhat easterly into Ganges. Upon the bank of this river stand the castle, one of the fairest and admirablest building of the East, some three or four miles in compasse, inclosed with a faire and strong wall of squared stone; about which is cast a faire ditch, over it draw-bridges...adjoining to the ditch without the citie are very large suburbs. The city and suburbs are one way seven mile in length, three in breadth. The noblemen's and merchants' houses built with bricke and stone, are flat roofed; the common sort, of muddle walls, covered with thatch which cause often and terrible fires. The citie hath six gates. The adjoining river Gemini being broader than the Thames at London, on which are many boats, some of one hundred tunnes but these cannot returne against the streame. Most of the noblemen's houses are by the riverside.'[18]

During the reign of Akbar, Mirza Ghiyas Beg, an impoverished Persian nobleman from Isfahan left his homeland to seek fortune in Hindustan. Accompanied by his family, including his pregnant wife, he made his way across treacherous mountain passes and on the way, they stopped in Kandahar

Top: Marble jalis or screens exemplify
the great craft traditions of India used
then both as practical screening
for the zenanas and for purely
aesthetic reasons.

Left: The image of India is inextricably
linked to this monument, in its breadth
as much as in its detail. Every inch of the
Taj Mahal today is deeply studied as it
faces the changes being wrought in the
city. Changes which were to alter Agra
forever began soon after Shah Jahan
shifted his capital to Delhi.

MAN BURJ, AGRA FORT

CARVED PANEL OVER CENTRAL DOORWAY

Above and facing page: The inlay and carving at Musamman Burj, drawn by 19th-century engineers and archivists in immense and accurate detail, reflect how important this section of Shah Jahan's palaces are.

Right above: Jahangir Mahal reflects the synthesis of cultures and architectural styles which defined Akbar's style of architecture. Jahangir and Shah Jahan subsequently also contributed to the grandeur of this fort. The impressive architectural styles of this complex are a rare amalgamation of the aesthetic sensibilities of the different Mughal emperors who were greatly influenced by the design aesthetic of the lands they had conquered.

Left: The Agra Fort is distinctive for its massive protective wall, some 70-feet high and 1 ½ miles in circumference, and dressed in red sandstone. Encircled by a moat. The fort stands high above the city, its ramparts defining the skyline, its eminence reinforced, with each generation making new additions to its already elegant architecture. Its entrance gateway is particularly impressive in scale, especially as it was continuously built upon.

where in 1577, she gave birth to Meherunissa – Light Among Women. Ghiyas Beg appeared at the Court of Akbar, who vastly impressed with him. Within two decades, Akbar placed him as officer in charge of the imperial buildings in Agra Fort. In time, Beg built a mansion befitting his position at court on the riverfront as well as a garden across as did all noblemen of the time.

Beg's daughter Meherunissa lived with him in Agra, and although she had been married earlier, Jahangir was so besotted with her that he married her in 1611 in an ostentatious ceremony, and renamed her Nur Jahan – Light of

82

SAMMAN BURJ, AGRA FORT

DETAIL OF INLAID BRACKETS

SAMMAN BURJ, AGRA FORT

DETAIL OF INLAID PANELS

SCALE OF FEET

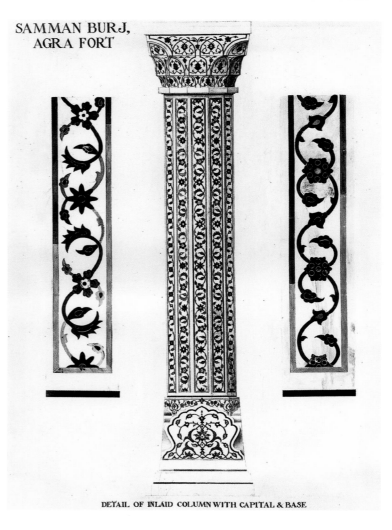

SAMMAN BURJ, AGRA FORT

DETAIL OF INLAID COLUMN WITH CAPITAL & BASE

the World. The next year, Ghiyas Beg celebrated the birth of his granddaughter Arjumand Banu – Respected Princess – the future wife of Shah Jahan and the legendary Mumtaz Mahal – Chosen One of the Palace. Nur Jahan and Mumtaz Mahal rose to be the most powerful women in the Mughal Empire.

Ghiyas Beg now was Itimad-ud-Daulah, Prime Minister to Jahangir, and wielded enormous power, largely through his daughter Nur Jahan, wife of Jahangir and Empress of Hindustan. In time, his son Asaf Khan, Mumtaz Mahal's father grew equally powerful when he became Shah Jahan's father-in-law. Itimad-ud-Daulah died in 1622, shortly after the death of his wife. Both Jahangir and Nur Jahan were grief-stricken, and Jahangir was now so weakened by decades of addiction to wine and opium that he decided to move to his beloved Kashmir Valley, seeking peace in his tranquil garden. In 1627, a few days after a hunting accident, he died at the age of 58 in a *serai* a few hundred yards off the imperial highway in the Kashmir Valley, and was taken to Lahore to be buried.

Above: Jahangir's wife Nur Jahan, Light of the World, Empress of India, held immense sway over the affairs of the state as well as exercised control over trade and business. In this portrait she is shown in relatively simple jewels, with a headdress almost the same as the one worn by the Emperor, and holding a cup of wine.

Above left: A nobleman at the court of Jahangir, attributed to Balchand in the early 17th century.

Facing page: Jahangir seated on the throne, with Asaf Khan and his son Shaista Khan (2nd and 1st from right, respectively). In Jahangir's time, Asaf Khan's father, Itimad-ud-Daulah, was the emperor's most powerful Prime Minister. Later, Asaf Khan, Mumtaz Mahal's father, wielded immense influence in the court of Shah Jahan.

Below and facing page: After Jahangir died, Nur Jahan devoted herself to the construction of the tomb of Ghiyas Beg or Itimad-ud-Daulah, her father and Prime Minister of Hindustan. Arguably one of the finest funerary structures in Hindustan, it had a seminal influence on the future the Taj Mahal, even outshining Emperor Akbar's Sikandra. Itimad-ud-Daulah had already begun to build his wife's tomb when he too died. Nur Jahan devoted herself to building this monument for her parents.

The tomb of Itimad-ud-Daulah was heavily embellished with stone inlay, creating a rich surface quite unique for its time. The stone was acquired from as far as Jaisalmer. A rich amalgam of inlay and painting in the interiors are reflective of Ghiyas Baig's Persian origins and the influence he brought to the court of Jahangir.

ITIMAD-UD-DAULAH

By the time Jahangir died, Nur Jahan had already embarked on a devotion which would result in one of the finest funerary structures in Hindustan and be a seminal influence on the future Taj Mahal, outshining the elegant Sikandra, designed by Akbar but embellished by Jahangir to honour his father. It would also herald the end of her powerful reign in Hindustan as Asaf Khan her brother, and his son-in-law Shah Jahan came to power.

To honour the memory of her father as the last Persian Prime Minister of Hindustan, Nur Jahan built Ghiyas Beg's or Itimad-ud-Daulah's tomb in his pleasure garden, on the banks of the Yamuna almost opposite the fort. His influence in the courts of Jahangir and Shah Jahan had been immense, and

contributed to the Persian refinements in the culture of the court, reflecting in the elegantly rendered tomb. Itmad-ud-Daulah's wife, who predeceased him, is buried at the centre of the tomb and he was later interred alongside, perhaps a precedent for the protocol followed at the Taj Mahal.

The garden is enclosed with high walls and on the western side on the riverfront, is an elegant pavilion on a raised terrace. The river, then pristine, would have flowed alongside, and would have been busy with barges of other nobles and even of the emperor. The riverside pavilion and the two side ones are richly decorated and inlaid with stylised carafes and wine cups. Clearly an evening spent here was one of easy comfort and libation, and its reuse as a funerary site did not stipulate changing these details.

The tomb at the centre of the *char bagh* is at the intersection of the water channels, diverted to flow around the square building that has the graves of the Beg family below the main level and a cenotaph on the ground floor. The distinctive feature of this tomb is undoubtedly the marble and inlay embellishments. Regarded as the building which marks the transition from the austere use of sandstone to the more luxurious use of inlay in marble, it is arguably the touchstone for a new Mughal architectural style.

The choice of using marble for surface cladding was not a first as Hoshang Shah's tomb at Mandu was also built in white marble, but here it is a more elegant building, richly embellished in *pietra dura*. 'The walls are inlaid with geometric as well as flowing patterns. Arabesques fill the spandrels over the arched recesses framing the doorways and geometric latticed windows. Inlaid *dado*s give way to the upper walls which are carved as well as ornamented with cypresses, cups, jugs and *guldasta*s – symbols of celebration and pleasure. The interior of its roof is elaborated with incised painted and gilded stucco. The cenotaphs themselves are in a rich gold-coloured marble known as *khattu*.'[19] Delicately carved marble screens allow the interiors to be gently lit by a play of dappled sunlight, further adding to the abundance and harmony of the design. It is, in fact, this harmonisation that makes the tomb of Itmad-ud-Daulah, Nur Jahan's most lasting legacy.

Following pages: The ceiling of the tomb of Itimad-ud-Daulah is as elaborate as the rest of the monument. The paintings made with crushed semi-precious stones, still retain their lustre.

Once, the waterfront of Agra was defined by no less than 44 gardens, largely lost today, while the gardens which became tomb-gardens, still remain. Of these, a noteworthy surviving one is the tomb-garden believed to be of Afzal Khan, a literary adventurer of the 17th century. A native of Shiraz,

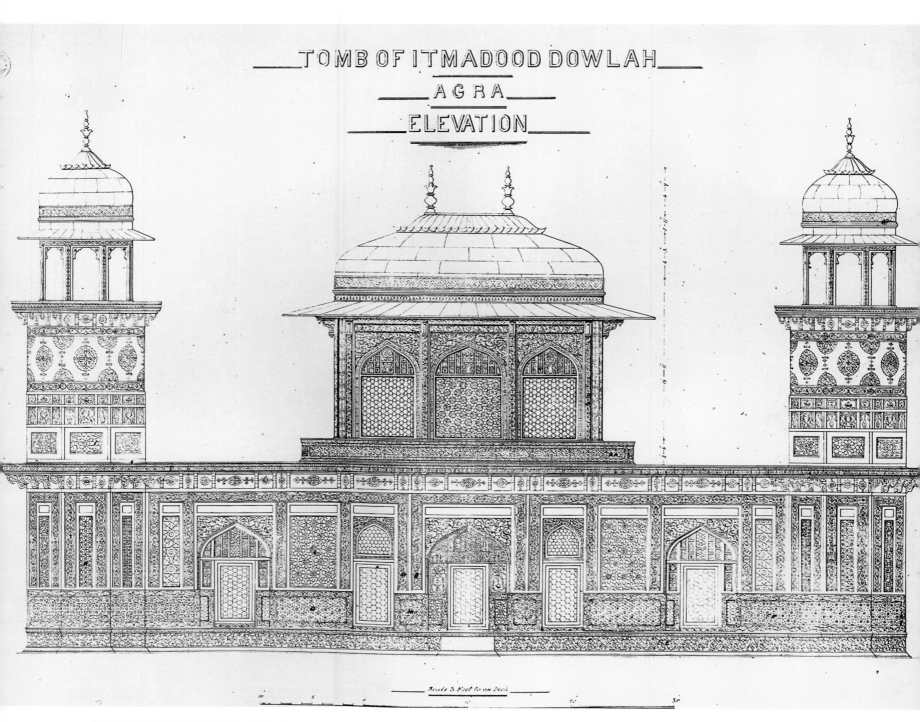

TOMB OF ITMADOOD DOWLAH
AGRA
ELEVATION

Scale 5 Feet to an Inch

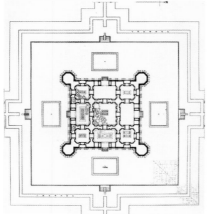

Above and facing page: Detailed drawings of the monuments of Agra undertaken by British engineers in the early 19th century such as these of the tomb of Itimad-ud-Daulah and the Taj Mahal are invaluable to present day researchers as they provide benchmarks for new work.

Following pages: The drawing of the exterior of Itimad-ud-Daulah is one of the finest renderings in the ASI. Each detail is remarkably reproduced and in some cases perhaps with some creativity as the façade shows more brilliant use of colour with reds and blues instead of the elegant muted shades of natural stone used here.

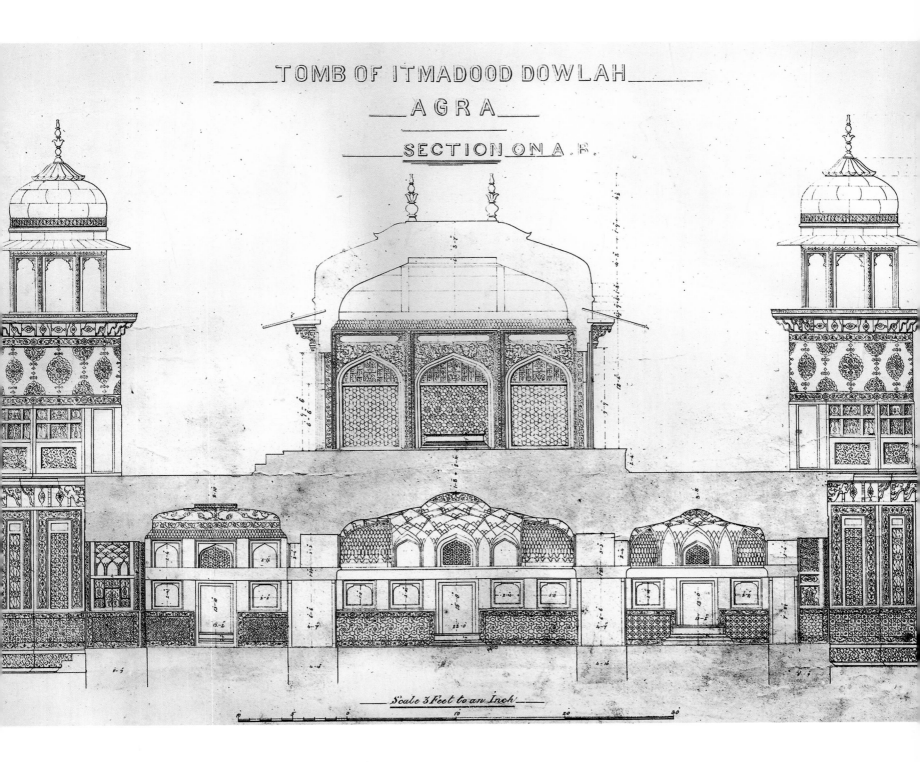

TOMB OF ITMADOOD DOWLAH
AGRA
SECTION ON A. B.

Scale 3 Feet to an Inch

Pages 94-95: The tomb is a square building with the graves of the Prime Minister and his wife in an exotic stone khattu. At the upper level are the cenotaphs. The distinctive features of this tomb are undoubtedly the marble and inlay embellishments.

It is regarded as the building which marks the transition from the austere use of sandstone to the more luxurious use of marble, and arguably the touchstone for a new Mughal architectural style.

Above, top and right bottom: Mulla Shukrullah as-Shirazi was an Iranian nobleman of Persian descent who left his native Shiraz in 1608, to come to the court of Jahangir and was given the title Allami as-Shirazi. His tomb garden, Chini ka Rauza, stands out amidst the other structures along the River Yamuna in Agra, because of its alignment – it is oriented to face Mecca rather than the river edge, reflective of the piety in the tomb plan.

Facing page: The interior of Chini ka Rauza is as heavily embellished as its exterior. Wall paintings enrich the high-vaulted ceiling. The building is distinctive not only for its tile work but it is also built in the Sultanate style with simpler arches and a dome.

he was originally named Shukrullah, and came through Surat to Burhanpur, from where he entered the service of Jahangir and was given the title 'Allami as-Shirazi' (Very Wise One from Shiraz). A successful courtier even through Shah Jahan's reign, he then became Diwan-i-Kul or Finance Minister.

Shirazi was an aristocrat with refined tastes that he brought to the court in poetry, astronomy, mathematics, and was said to be held in high esteem by Shah Jahan. His tomb-garden was located at the heart of Mughal Agra, reflecting his eminence in the hierarchy of nobility. This came to be known as Chini ka Rauza and is unique in that it is situated at an angle to the river, distinctly deviating from the classical tomb-garden layout and the symmetries of the Mughal gardens. In fact, it is aligned to Mecca, signifying a more orthodox design conforming to Islamic tenets.

The tomb was once at the centre of a walled *char bagh*, of which only the riverfront *burjs* survive. It is a simple square structure with a Sultanate-style dome with *pishtaqs* projecting slightly upwards and partially concealing the dome, built in the traditional *hasht bihisht* plan with eight rooms around the central chamber. Each bay has a large *pishtaq* and small columns at each corner, projecting upwards as minarets. The tomb is situated on a platform with vaulted chambers that have since been sealed.

The distinctive feature of this tomb is the façade covered in patterned polychrome mosaics with flowering plants in lobed arches and calligraphy. This tile work is typically used in Persian architecture and is also seen in Shah Jahan's buildings in Lahore. It is perhaps the lavish use of tiles which has given it the colloquial name, 'Chini ka Rauza'. Nearby, and once in the same *char bagh*, is the tomb of Afzal Khan, a nobleman at Shah Jahan's court. Afzal Khan died in Lahore in 1639 at the age of 70 and is said to have been buried in the tomb he had built for himself. The interior of Afzal Khan's tomb has elaborate vaulted ceiling with painted stucco work, today a mere shadow of its former elegance.

Left and below: The distinctive feature of this particular tomb is that the façade is entirely covered with polychrome mosaics in wonderful patterns, with flowering plants in lobed arches and calligraphy. This tile work on the façade is what is typically used in Persian architecture, with patterns of flowering plants and calligraphic inscriptions also seen in Shahjahani buildings in Lahore.

Facing page: Chini ka Rauza was extensively damaged in the 1922 floods, with an entire section of its façade sheared off, leaving its outer chambers exposed to the elements.

Shah Jahan, Emperor of the World, was born under the most auspicious astrological circumstances – the conjunction of two planets: Jupiter and Venus. Known throughout his life as the Second Lord of the Auspicious Conjunction, the first having been his ancestor Timur, the destiny of the emperor was ordained. Shah Jahan inherited the title of Emperor at the age of 36. It was a much contested throne and he dealt with his siblings in keeping with what was believed to be the culture of the Timurids – he sent an envoy with a message: 'It would be well at this time when the heavens were troubled and the earth seditious, that Dawar Baksh and the other princes were made wanderers in the plains of non-existence.'[20] Shah Jahan ensured the end of any opposition to his throne as all possible contenders 'were all sent out of this world.'[21]

He commanded an immense expanse of land, uniting Hindustan from Kabul to Bengal, and as far south directly or indirectly as the River Kaveri in what he hoped would be an era of peace and prosperity. Mandelslo, from the court of the Duke of Holstein who, in 1633, dispatched an embassy to the Great Duke of Muscovy and the King of Persia, wrote amongst the early accounts of the city, though his account didn't include the Taj Mahal which was already being built. He said it was one of the noblest cities of Hindustan and which the Mughals enjoyed immensely. He described the city streets as fair and spacious, and some of them vaulted, of almost a mile in length. Each was distinguished by its merchandise as every trade and every merchant had a street or quarter. He felt that there were at least 80 *caravanserais* for foreign merchants, some three-storeys high and of a high standard with storehouse stables and lodgings well laid out. The city was further dignified with at least 70 great mosques and over 800 *hammams* or public baths.

He saw numerous palaces of the rajas and lords, and, chiefest of all, the imperial palace, fortified with a moat and drawbridge. The jealously guarded treasure was estimated on credible authority at above fifteen hundred million crowns, or over £300,000,000. Mandelslo further described Agra as a very densely inhabited city at this time, so extensive and populous that he thought that if it were required, an army of two hundred thousand men could easily be raised. He was of the view that the entire eastern world had business in Agra. There was a levy of ten per cent he wrote, on all trade in or out of the city. Equally, he believed there was probably no nation in the east which did not have trade in the city.

Facing page: This portrait of Shah Jahan exemplifies his supremacy as Emperor of the World as he stands on top of the globe. His position is further strengthened by the celestial umbrella protecting him and his crown is proffered from the heavens. The merger of the spiritual and the temporal could be perceived here as complete.

Above: Sultan Khurram, c. 1615, before he became Emperor of the World.

The palaces of Agra Fort built by Shah Jahan in pristine white marble with gilded cupolas rising above the massive red sandstone fortifications are delicate as well as imperial – a style which Shah Jahan introduced here, transforming Emperor Akbar's forbidding sandstone palaces. The balance of the mass of the fort walls and the delicacy of the gold topped domes are what makes Shajahani architecture so unique.

François Bernier, a physician attached to the Mughal court from 1659 to 1665, also wrote about the city at the time: 'Agra having been a favourite and more frequent abode of the Kings of Hindoustan since the days of Akbar, by whom it was built and named Akbarabad, it surpasses Delhi in extent, in the multitude of residences belonging to *omrahs* and rajas, and of the good stone or brick houses inhabited by private individuals and in the number and convenience of its Karuanas-serrahs. Agra has also to boast of two celebrated mausoleums...it is however, without walls and inferior in some respect to the other capital; for not having been constructed after any settled design, it wants the uniform and wide streets that so eminently distinguish Delhi. Four or five of the streets, where trade is the principal occupation, are of great length and the houses tolerably good; nearly all the others are short, narrow and irregular and full of windings and corners: the consequence is that when the court is at Agra, there is often a strange confusion...'[22]

Agra was at its peak, it was peacetime and the emperor held sway across Hindustan. By now, the waterfront of Agra had developed significantly. It was dominated by the fort, capped

with Shah Jahan's white marble cupolas and domes, but all around, the city had grown exponentially into a sophisticated urban hub. The river was bound by gardens of pure pleasure while on the side of the fort, there were grand mansions. These mansions and the gardens were symbols of power and patronage as they were given as *jagir*s to nobility by the emperor himself.

Shah Jahan's most significant legacy is undoubtedly extraordinary buildings of immense scale and elegance, never seen before or since. He built tombs, palaces, gardens, and embellished his ancestors' graves and gardens across the country. He oversaw the elegant tomb for his father at Lahore, sparing no cost for its completion. He provided marble screens around Babur's grave in Kabul. In Agra Fort, his refined tastes were evident as he added jewel-like mosques and marble palaces, replacing the forbidding dark red sandstone his grandfather Akbar so favoured. He renamed the city Akbarabad in honour of his grandfather to whom he owed his throne.

Asaf Khan, Shah Jahan's father-in-law, was appointed Chief Minister. He was the envy of all as Shah Jahan in an un-imperial way, visited his father-in-law at his mansion along the river, while Asaf Khan went through the observances of spreading

Following pages: This is the earliest extant plan of Agra city, with its 44 gardens flanking the river's edge. Popularly known as the Jaipur map, this shows details of the gardens, the structures within and clearly the intensity of building on both sides of the river. Nearer the Taj Mahal, shown on the lower left-hand side, the garden and havelis thin out. Beyond the fort in the centre of the map, the Jama Masjid can be seen as also a central road with large havelis on both sides.

103

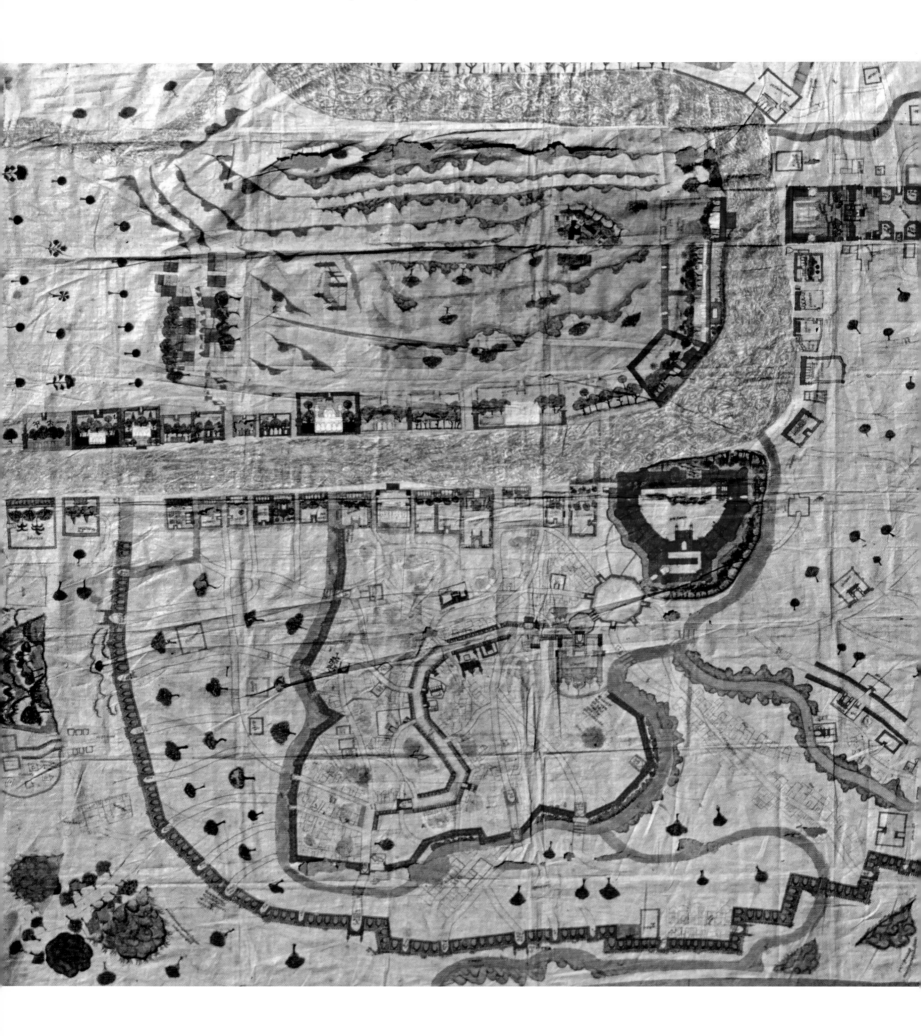

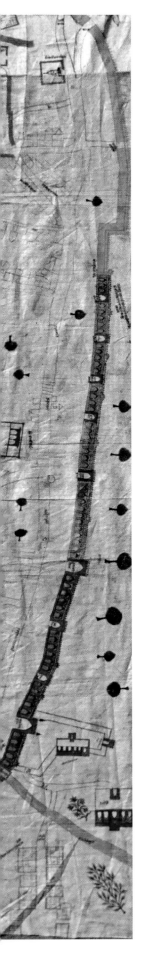

a carpet under His Majesty's feet and scattering money over his head.'[23] Horses, elephants and jewels were offered to Shah Jahan who stayed in the mansion, enjoying its festivities. Undoubtedly, Asaf Khan's mansion would have been the grandest. It would have had many courtyards and many layers of outer and inner chambers, some leading to secluded walled gardens and others overlooking the waterfront and benefiting from the cool air of the river. The gardens inside too would have had fountains and water channels heated in winter and cool in summer. It is believed that among others, Asaf Khan's mansion too was probably demolished in 1857 after India's First War of Independence as the then imperial rulers sought to establish themselves, obliterating any remnants of the *omrah*.

Most of the mansions had *tehkhanas* which were also fed with little water channels to provide a cool retreat during the searing heat and dust of summer. The interiors too would have been embellished with paintings, inlays, and furnished with tapestries and carpets now made in Agra. Conditions in the early 17th century were described by Francisco Pelsaert in a report to the Dutch East India Company during his seven years in Agra from 1620 to 1627: '...After passing the Fort, there is the Nakhas, a great market, where in the morning horses, camels, oxen, tents, cotton goods, and many other things are sold. Beyond it lie the houses of some great lords, such as Mirza Abdulla, son of Khan Azam (3000 horse); Aga Nur, provost of the King's army (3000 horse); Jahan Khan (2000 horse) ; Mirza Khurram son of Khan Azam (2000 horse); Mahabat Khan (8000 horse); Khan Alam (5000 horse); Raja Bet [?] Singh I (3000 horse); the late Raja Man Singh (5000 horse); Raja Madho Singh (2000 horse). Each was a powerful noble at the court of the emperor.'[24] The nobles' houses extended over a mile south-east, up to Mahabat Khan's garden-mansion. After the collapse of the Mughals, these were probably all looted.

To sustain the city at this scale, there was a huge trading community. Craftsmen would have flocked to the city to carve and inlay the palaces as they were being redeveloped. Carpet weavers from Persia were amongst the many traders and craftsmen who followed the Mughals to Hindustan, and who flourished under the emperors. Under Nur Jahan's patronage, carpet weaving attained great excellence as she commissioned finer and richer products. Replicated from miniature paintings, these works were often believed to be the Mughals' finest creations. Renowned across Europe, these were soon exported to the courts of European royalty and remain, to this day, a

Above: The Jaipur Map details out as no other map does each garden and house before the destruction of Agra altered this vocabulary completely.

105

Below: Agra Fort has always been inspirational in size and scale. Its fortifications rise some 70 feet and dominate the skyline with cuppolas, pavilions and palaces, often intensely and creatively detailed. Company paintings such as this one, reflect the importance given to recording monuments. However, paintings such as these are often not entirely authentic as elements like the waterfront baradari *are clearly an addition introduced perhaps from another site.*

Facing page: Shah Jahan's court was elaborate and had established hierarchies for attendance. He was not as inclusive as his grandfather and so controlled his kingdom with much more stringent protocols. Visitors from across Europe and beyond flocked to the court of the emperor, making Agra a bustling metropolitan city that conducted international business.

major craft tradition in Agra even though royal patronage has been replaced by compulsions of commerce and export.

Shah Jahan was more orthodox than his father and grandfather. He discontinued Jahangir's practice of prostrating before the emperor as un-Islamic. He was not as tolerant or inclusive as Akbar and ordered the demolition of newly built temples. Over time, though, he grew more liberal, and writers, poets and musicians of all dispositions were welcomed at his court. Peace, however, was short-lived, and the north-west of the empire was once again vulnerable, the result of an incomplete campaign in Kandahar in his father's time. More worryingly, there was fresh trouble in the Deccan. Shah Jahan followed Aurangzeb on his march south. He placed his armies under Aurangzeb's command to try and bring some resolution in the Deccan while he marched behind with his imperial cavalcade at a statelier pace.

Campaigns to the Deccan meant long stretches away from the court and raising armies at a huge cost. The entire court moved with him, a huge convoy of elephants, horses, royal processions, tents, carpets, kitchens, servants and stragglers – almost a sea of humanity crossing the lands of Hindustan, but barely covering 10 *kos* a day. The camps of a scale Abul Fazl described in Akbar's time took 100 elephants, 500 camels and more to transport…one camp opening before the other closed.

While Agra Fort had been built by the Lodis on the river, guaranteeing access to water, control of trade and as a natural barrier on at least one side of the fort, it was consolidated by successive Mughal emperors who embellished and gave it its present form. With the consolidation of their power, the city and their own habitation, they could now engage more easily

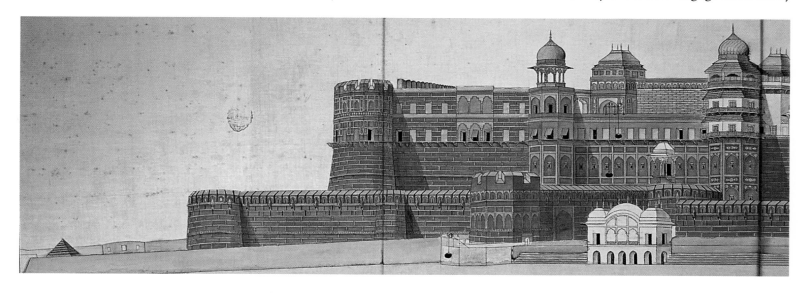

Facing pace: A fine Mughal carpet shows an abundance of flowers, thus ensuring that there was as much natural beauty inside the palaces as in the great gardens. Carpet-weaving was at its apogée during Jahangir's reign when Nur Jahan owned the largest weaving centres. During her reign, carpets, one of Agra's most famous craft, were exported through the many traders who came to Agra to buy them. To this day, Agra is well known for its carpet-manufacturing skills although now hand-crafted carpets have been largely overshadowed by the industrial ones.

Left: Elephant-fighting was a favoured sport of the emperors and there was always a tract of land between the fort and the river so that the emperor could watch elephant fights for pleasure. Akbar went so far as to pit his sons against each other; the winner would briefly find greater favour with his father. This cruel sport is wonderfully rendered here and shows the emperor watching from his pavilion at the top while the nobility is gathered below.

with the broader landscapes that they colonised. Thus, they were quick to understand the potential of the river not just as a system of mobility or vital transport but one which could also be harnessed to mould and construct the landscape for their own pleasure and well-being.

As part of this development, the first garden was arguably Aram Bagh, Babur's creation, fuelled by his distaste of Hindustan, steeped in nostalgia for the great *bagh*s of Kabul and Samarkand. In Central Asia, gardens were great symbols of power as Timur's ring of gardens in Samarkand were named after the great cities he conquered – Cairo, Damascus, Baghdad, Sultaneyah and Shiraz *bagh*s defined the conquered landscape. Babur's descriptions of these gardens are not only their best records but also reflect his own zeal for walled gardens.

By the 15th century though, the lavish Timurid Mongol culture was replaced by the growing piety of Islamic laws, and urban institutions were embraced, especially in Persian courts. These gardens were rich in political symbolism, developed by the ruling classes and secluded behind high walls. From Herat, Kabul and then India, gardens were the most desirable assets of the ruling elite. Royal houses and their nobles publically embraced the political and social context but behind these public expressions of faith, gardens were private and exclusive areas behind high walls, insulated from the public and the tawdriness of everyday affairs. Inside the four walls, was a life of great opulence and often, excess.

The concept of the *char bagh* as a garden of paradise is far removed from the Islamic belief that *jannat* awaits those who follow the path of Allah; *jannat* as a garden was quite clearly a more earthly version. The association with *jannat* in the other and much earlier *char bagh*s, could shift seamlessly from the luxurious life within to the creation of temporal and spiritual power centres. Either way, they represented power or, as Mughal gardens scholar, James Westcoat says, 'They were microcosms of spatial order within a more tumultuous and uncertain landscape.'[25] In *Rethinking the Islamic Garden,* Prof. Attillio Petroculli says, gardens had a deeper impact: 'Neglecting the Indo-Muslim city of Agra on the right bank of the river, Babur decided to settle on the opposite side, building a regular pattern of gardens in the manner of those of Lahore and Dholpur, stretching for more than a kilometre, in which the idea of "monumentality" and "representation" of the new order was entrusted to the high, continuous stone plinth along the river. This pattern ended up establishing a framework for future urban development.'[26]

Right: The famous painting of a garden party by Humayun, of which mere fragments survive, evokes the lavish lifestyle of the time. An abundance of food is brought to this party attended by a large number of guests as well as servants who remain on the periphery of the event. A beautiful garden, with flowering trees surrounds the emperor's pavilion.

Below: A 17th-century game board decorated with a floral pattern serves to highlight how important the flower garden was in the Mughal imagination.

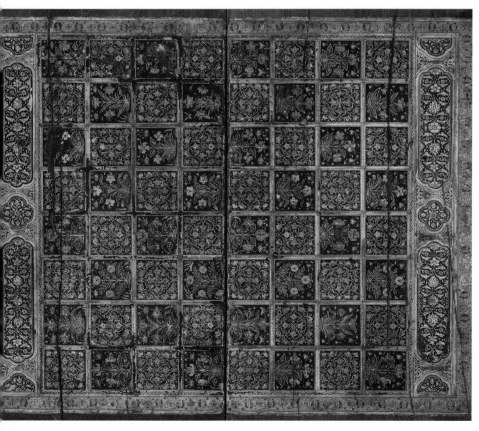

It was, therefore, not merely the joy of fruit and flowers which mandated these gardens but a retreat from the reality of what they professed and imposed in public. In Hindustan, the gardens along the riverfront at Agra were assigned by royal decree, often as *jagir*s – Babur's Aram Bagh was given to Nur Jahan as her *jagir* by Jahangir. At their peak, when there were 44 gardens, access to the river would have been exclusive. Moreover, the development of riverfront gardens by the Mughals in Agra also marks a departure from the 'simple common sense' principles used elsewhere in Hindustan; they harnessed the river with massive raised terraces on the opposite side of the city, redefining the relationship of the city and its lifeline – the river. These platforms defined the edge of the river and secured it from its otherwise violent sways.

It is arguably for this reason that in this stretch of its flow in Agra, the Yamuna has not changed course for centuries as its edges were trained by the massive walls of the pleasure gardens that lined it.

The Mughal layout of the city was unique. It flanked the river on both sides; gardens on the east bank and on the western

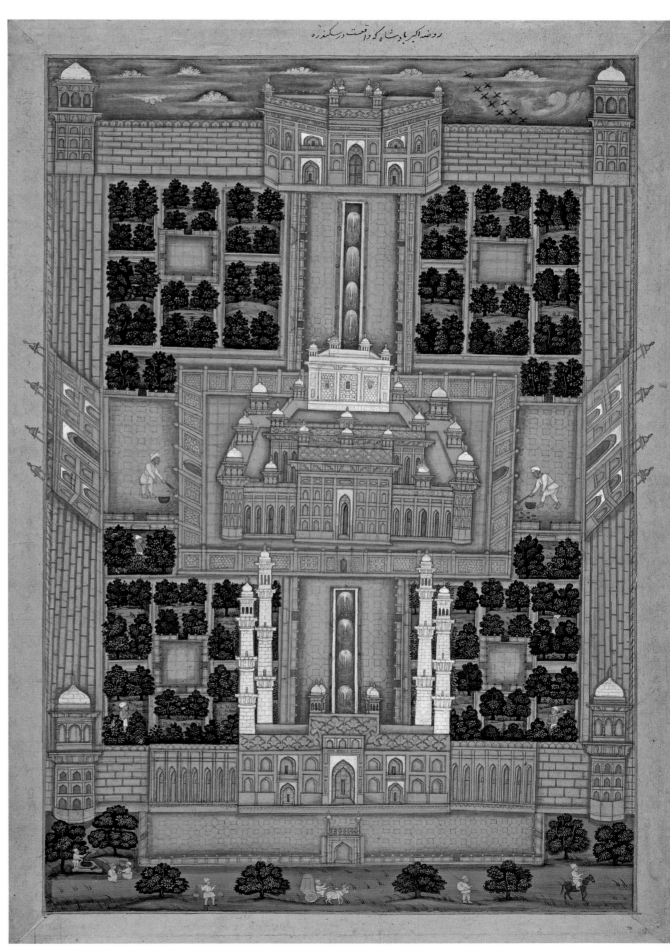

روضه اکبر پادشاه که واقعست در سکندره

Right: This early painting of Sikandra shows the perfect symmetry of the garden, with the tomb in the centre as a classical char bagh. *The presence of large trees is important as it shows how the layout of the garden was visualised.*

side were part of the great mansions of Mughal nobility. As each Mughal emperor consolidated his empire and an era of peace was ushered in, possibly nobility found it desirable to move out of the rigid formality of the fort and build their grand mansions along the riverfront. Here, they too were assured of the cool air of the river, of terraces from where they could view river traffic in privacy as well as develop gardens with ease as water was so readily available. These great houses were built on a hierarchy as various emperors assigned mansions to their favoured nobles.

The *char baghs* across the river, a mere boat ride away – few 'outsiders' had access either to the emperor as Head of State or the emperor in his pleasure gardens – were as much a continuation of Babur's nostalgia for Samarkand as they were of the Timurid culture which he brought to Hindustan. Mortimer Wheeler, on the other hand, writes that the Mughal transition into formal structured gardens was a response to the disordered landscape of Hindustan. The riverfront garden in Agra was as unique to the principles of city development in Hindustan as the garden's layout itself.

The Mughals built great mosques and tombs as well as palaces and forts. For each of these, the garden provided the canvas for the imagery, and central to this was flowing fresh water to sustain them, their *hammam*s and, eventually, their pleasure gardens. Immense gateways intimidated the local population. The riverfront was appropriated by nobility and the citizens of Agra lived behind these mansions, dependent on tanks and pools of stagnant water.

Equally, the siting and setting of the gardens was an adaptation to the environment as the garden-palaces were now oriented towards the river instead of the cardinal directions. They were also a direct contrast to the structures of the great historic cities of Mathura and Vrindavan where the landscape was structured more loosely on a different set of cultural narratives. What emerged in Agra along the river was unambiguously a new cultural landscape, a landscape that also evolved more abruptly than its counterparts that evolved more gently, with shifting interpretations and readings of the narratives that informed their structure. In the case of the pleasure gardens along the river at Agra, a mix of policy, legislation and subversive tactics by their custodians would result in their maintenance but also their destruction over time as, unlike the gardens at Mathura and Vrindavan, these places were never central to the public imagination.

Facing page: The palace is a city within a city, with access only to the king and his nobility. The zenana *complex for the concubines is the central feature. This is where the emperor retreated for leisure, so these complexes became more and more elaborate with* char baghs, *waterways, fountains, flowers and fruit gardens. In sharp contrast is the imagery of war, battles, arms and armies in the distance.*

Above: This painting from the Baburnama *or* Tuzk-e-Babri, *attributed to the artist Sur Gujarati, depicts Babur celebrating the birth of his son Humayun in 1508 in a* char bagh *in Kabul.*

روز آذر نهم دی ماه الهی موافق روز جمعه دویم ربیع الثانی نقسیم غرصیت مدارا الخلافه اکره نمودند وازراه دریای چون

برکشتی سوار دولت شده توجه فرمودند اعیان سلطنت وارکان دولت بمقدارکنجانیس کشتیها وزورقها سامان و

آرایش داده متوجه کشتند واردوی بزرگ ازراه خشکی متوجهان سمت کشت وروز فروردین نوز دهم

دی ماه الهی موافق دوشنبه دوازد سیم ربیع الثانی دارالخلافه اکره مستقر رایات جلال شد

2

Reimagining the Taj Mahal
The Emperor's View

Facing page: Akbar leaving the Agra Fort in his barge, accompanied by a large retinue of nobility on other barges is indicative of a time when the emperor's movements were elaborate undertakings.

In 1631, on their way to the Deccan, shortly after arriving in Burhanpur, Mumtaz Mahal gave birth to Husnara Begum, her 13th child, who lived for just a few days. By now, Mumtaz had given birth to seven sons, of whom four survived, and six daughters, of whom only two lived. Husnara's death did not bode well. In these forlorn times, Mumtaz Mahal was once again pregnant – with her 14th child. She was 40 and did not survive the ordeal.

There are many tragic accounts of the time, especially court accounts of doom and desperation, not least of Shah Jahan 'shedding tears like rain water.'[1] There is also the legend of Mumtaz Mahal's dying wishes – on her hearing the child's cry from within her womb and knowing she would not survive, it is believed she summoned the emperor, and in her dying breath, while securing the rights of her surviving children, is also believed to have said: 'You should build over me such a mausoleum that the like of it may not be seen anywhere else in the world.'[2] Official accounts describe Shah Jahan's grief as a heartbreak which 'the discerning eye of the world-conquering king was flooded with tears.'[3] He buried her at Zainabad, opposite the fort at Burhanpur from where he could see her grave. The court was placed in mourning and the emperor withdrew from public appearances. When he finally emerged, 'the hair on his beard had turned white.'[4] He would devote the next decade of his life to frenzied building, which, while cathartic, marked the beginning of the end of the Mughal Empire.

Above: Man Singh received the title of Mirza Raja from Akbar. In 1605, Man Singh became a mansabdar *of 7,000 or a cavalry of 7,000 in the Mughal forces. He fought many important campaigns for Akbar, most notably against Rana Pratap, and was Akbar's most trusted general, a position he lost under Jahangir.*

Dressed in white muslin, the emperor set the tone for the court in mourning for several years. Six months after her death, Mumtaz's son Shah Shuja, accompanied by her physician Wazir Khan and her closest friend, Satiunissa, disinterred her body from Zainabad and journeyed with it to Agra, arriving a month later, in January 1632. Shah Jahan remained in Burhanpur as he was still engaged in the Deccan. It was a year after Mumtaz Mahal's death that he returned to his capital to embark on a project that would take 22 years, and consume both the emperor and his empire.

Shah Jahan's priority was to acquire land for a mausoleum that would be as worthy of his wife as his stature. On either side of the fort were the great mansions of nobility including the one of his father-in-law, Asaf Khan, Raja Todar Mal's *baradari*, and the great *char bagh*s of nobility on the other side of the river. Finally, he selected land some distance from the fort, on the bend of the river, in a more rural environment. He acquired the land – the gardens of Raja Jai Singh of Amber, inherited from his grandfather Raja Man Singh, and one of Akbar's finest generals. Raja Jai Singh was compensated with four great mansions in the city.

According to records, the land was 'to the south side of the Abode of the Caliphate, and overlooking the Jumna, a tract of land or *zamini* which, formerly was the mansion of Raja Man Singh but at this time was in the occupation of his grandson Raja Jai Singh and which, from the point of view of his eminence and pleasantness, appeared to be worthy of the burial of that one whose residence is *jannat*.'[5] Lahauri records the transaction: 'And the Raja as a token of his sincerity and devotion, donated the said land and considered this to be a

Above: Burhanpur Fort on the banks of the Tapti was a major fort for Shah Jahan as it was from here that he launched his offensives into the Deccan. It was here that his beloved wife Mumtaz Mahal died while giving birth to her 14th child in 1631.

Below: Jaipur Map (detail).

source of happiness. However, His Majesty in exchange for that granted to the Raja a lofty house which belonged to the crown estate.'[6] Clearly, the transaction needed to be in accordance with the sacred endeavour of building *jannat,* and so ensured there were no mis-steps in the process. To an extent, the choice of this land was possibly inspired by the location of the grave opposite Burhanpur Fort where too was a great bend in the river and also Itimad-ud-Daulah's tomb which had attained great significance in terms of its elegant presence on the riverfront. However, the emperor had far greater ambitions to fulfil in his wife's supposed last wish for her *rauza.* Not only did the bend in the river propitiously allow for the mausoleum to be located, based on the classic four cardinal directions but it also allowed the grave to be correctly aligned to Mecca – two important reasons determining the choice of the site. The river was clearly at the centre of his vision and the concept would develop around that. The framing of the site from Akbarabad Fort (or Agra as it was known later), the extension of the site across the river and its strategic downriver views would have perhaps contributed to the decision to choose this precise location.

By the time the funeral procession arrived in Akbarabad, as the Abode of the Caliphate was known in January 1632, the land had been acquired, and construction of the *takht* had begun. Mumtaz Mahal was buried close to where she would ultimately be entombed. Kanbo noted in contemporary records that a small domed building was quickly erected so that no *na mahram* would be able to view her grave. The heavenly site was already bustling with workmen less than six months after her death.

Shah Jahan reached Akbarabad nearly a year after Mumtaz Mahal's death and an *urs* on her first death anniversary was held in her memory, marking the union of the soul with God. 'To insure greater rest and everlasting tranquillity of those who had taken up residence in the vicinity of divine mercy, they spend one whole night and day in observances.'[7] It is a service which continues to date, though perhaps more modestly than Shah Jahan's first *urs.*

The first *urs* was recorded as an impressive feast held in the south garden, with a lavish spread of food, beverages, dried fruits, sweetmeats and aromatic essences. Great tents were installed in the grounds of the grave, encircled by smaller tents, with a rigid hierarchy of seating – only aristocrats had access to the platform, while camel drivers and other such persons were sequestered farthest away. With princes and nobility in attendance, the *ulema,* the shiekhs and the *hafiz*

Above: Raja Jai Singh. The purchase of land from Raja Jai Singh was a matter of securing the perfect location for the mausoleum of his beloved wife in keeping with his vision. This also meant locating the mausoleum a little outside the city and was not only predicated by the reality that most of the riverfront around the fort was flanked on both sides by grand mansions and gardens of the nobility.

managed the event. With the ritual feasting, recitations from the Quran and the distribution of Rs 50,000 to the poor, the first death anniversary of Mumtaz Mahal was observed, first by the men, then by the women of the *zenana*. The *urs* also marked Shah Jahan's return to court after his extended period of mourning and, more importantly, his victories in the Deccan.

In keeping with Islamic custom that burial must take place below the ground, by the second *urs*, the *Padshahnama*[8] records that Mumtaz Mahal's body had been interred in its final resting place. This implies that the platform of the Taj Mahal, with its massive foundations some 30-feet high and 1,000-feet long was complete, as was the second platform of white marble. Awestruck by the scale of activities of the time, British traveller Peter Mundy noted in his eloquent records that 'there is alreadye about her tombe a raile of gold.'[9]

Muhamad Amin Qavini records: 'Forged out of more than forty thousand *tolas* of gold, cost equivalent to six hundred thousand rupees, it was brought...along with enamelled golden constellation orbs and hanging lamps for His Majesty's most enlightened inspection.'[10] He adds that its lamps would provide illumination for Jahanara and the ladies of the harem when they came for midnight prayers.

In 1643, 10 years later, the gold railing was removed, it was officially stated, to prevent theft but it was possibly capitalised

Above and facing page. The location and siting of the Taj was dictated by cardinal direction and here it achieves absolute north-south. It has the distinction of still being set away from the city, towering above the urban mass, arguably attaining sublime height and aspiration. The reality today is that the riverfront has a much more rural aspect as gardens have given way to nurseries and farming. Rigid controls on development have preserved the quality of environment around the Taj Mahal.

to fund the ongoing construction. In its place would soon stand an inlaid marble *jali* screen of great delicacy and exceptional craftsmanship.

In Islamic tradition, a grave should be open to the sky and the grave itself unadorned. In fact, the *ulema* cited two reasons to justify sheltering the grave or to protect it from weathering by plastering it over with gypsum. The universal practice of the *umma* from the earliest centuries has been building tombs over the graves of those celebrated for their piety so that they would be recognisable to pilgrims and visitors. For the majority of Muslims, especially in the subcontinent, the spiritual power derived from visiting the resting place of people of eminence or spiritual strength was significant. Over time, tomb complexes were viewed as an earthly perspective of *jannat*.

The construction and scale of a Mughal *rauza* was a statement of an emperor's power as seen, for instance, in Timur's magnificent fluted-domed tomb in Samarkand. Babur's grave in Kabul was more modest. Humayun's tomb in Delhi, which was built by Akbar, is notable as it marks an important transition from Timur's tomb in Samarkand to the Taj Mahal. These tombs were neither conservative, nor were they conformist, yet in every aspect, separately and collectively, the Taj was aspirational. The very height of the dome was path-breaking for its time, and was described as being heavenly in its ambition.

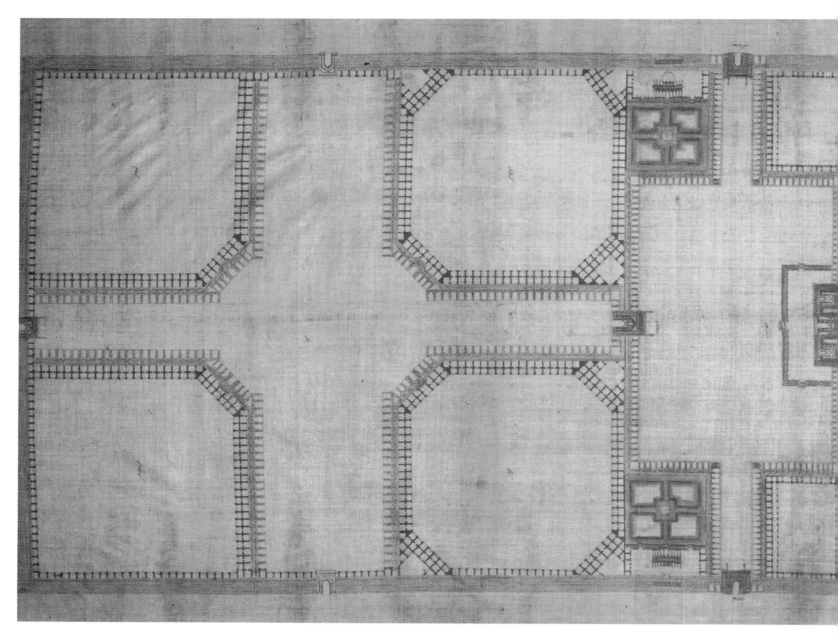

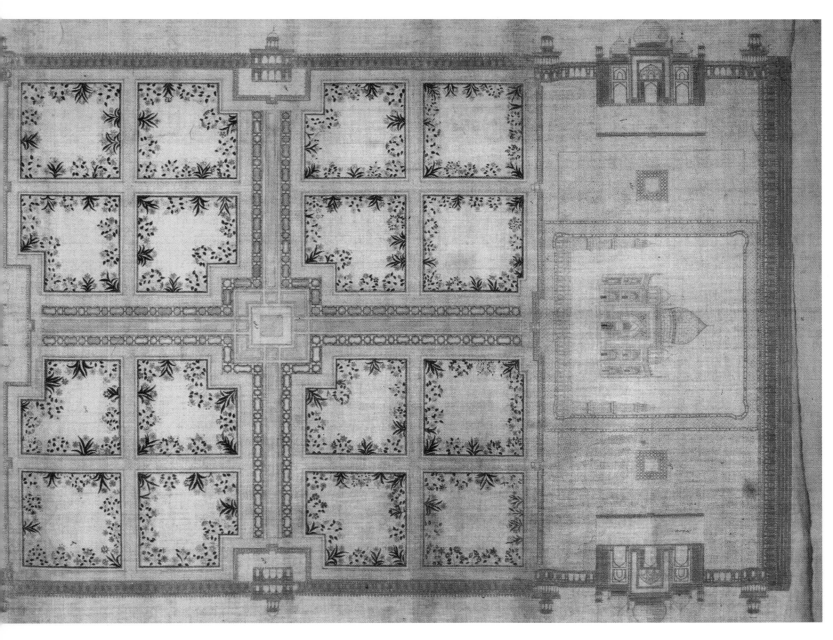

This plan from the Taj Mahal Museum is one of the earliest plans of the Taj Mahal that shows the entire complex with the walled garden. The mausoleum, mosque and Jawab are all on a platform along the river edge. South of the garden beyond the gateway lies the Jilau Khana, flanked by the khwasspuras as well as the lesser-known graves of Mumtaz Mahal's closest friends. The Jilau Khana marks the transitional space from the sacred to the secular Mumtazabad or Taj Ganj, as it is more popularly known today.

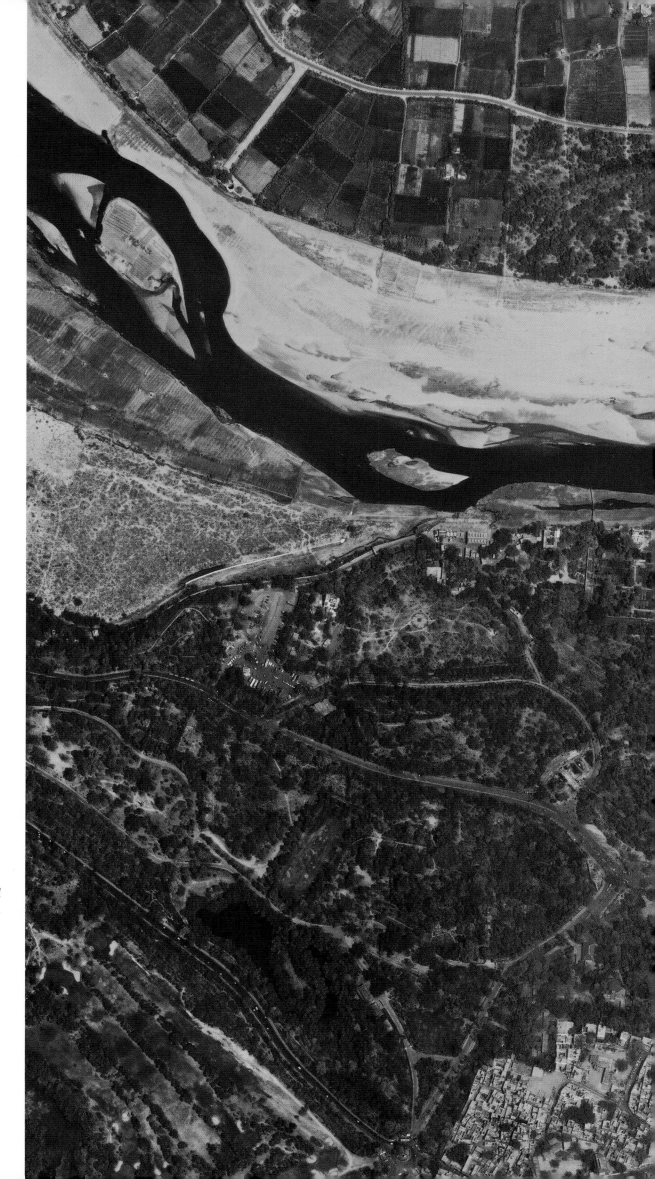

Right: The perfect alignment of the monument, its setting and Mehtab Bagh is clearly visible today. It is still possible to decipher the same grid in Taj Ganj, south of the main complex even though urbanisation is rapidly blurring the edges.

Following pages: The Taj Mahal appears to deviate from the classical char bagh as it is no longer at the centre of the garden but at one end, along the riverfront. Here, the concept has evolved with Shah Jahan appropriating the river as the ideal of "fresh-flowing water", and with Mehtab Bagh across, expands the entire plan of the char bagh across the river. The early drawing shows how clearly the mausoleum relates to Mehtab Bagh, the fort and the rest of the city.

ILLUMINED TOMB

The Taj Mahal – Illumined Tomb, it is believed, deviates from the classic design of being in the centre of a *char bagh*. Rather, it is situated on the waterfront at the far end of the *char bagh*. Ebba Koch believes this is the Mughal concept of a riverfront garden, developed specifically for Agra. Located at the river's edge, the Mughals developed the art of lifting water up from the river to the *char bagh* through an elaborate system of lifts, which fed the water channels and gardens, a system which was both practical and innovative for its time. Amongst others, Elizabeth Moynihan, a notable scholar proposes that, in fact, Mehtab Bagh, on the opposite bank of the Yamuna, was intended as part of the grand design of the Taj Mahal, with its reflecting pool as the focal point.

The Yamuna then would be the river of fresh and fast-flowing water. With the allegory of renewal, and with the tomb and graves in alignment with the cardinal directions, this attains even greater significance. If the Moonlight Garden to the north of the river is an integral part of the complex, then the mausoleum would be interpreted as being in the centre of a garden divided by the river, thus embracing the true ideal of *jannat* with fresh-flowing water and gardens filled with 'groves of shade...and fruit.'[11] If Shah Jahan envisaged this as *jannat,* then his cosmic alignments too are perfect: west-east flow the fresh waters of the Yamuna and north-south the principle canals of the two great *baghs*, and with the tomb at the centre, the symmetry is perfect. The size of the two *baghs* is the same, with the octagonal pond reflecting the Taj Mahal. 'When reflected in the river, the Taj Mahal as *axis mundi,* is transformed into an evanescent image above the crossing of the Four Rivers of Paradise. Only someone with Shah Jahan's vainglorious sense of himself could conceive such an audacious plan.'[12]

Unlike at Sikandra, or even the much smaller Itimad-ud-Daulah, where the water channels subdivide into smaller channels, at the Taj Mahal, there is a sanctity of the perfect cardinal orientation and layout which makes it distinctive.

The Taj Mahal was designed to be accessed by Shah Jahan and the royal family who only ever approached the mausoleum from his palace in the fort, by barge along the river. So his vision was circumscribed by this approach. The emperor's visits, too, would have been limited to salutations at the graves, with almost no perspective beyond. From the water, the 30-foot high elaborately patterned red sandstone wall towered above them.

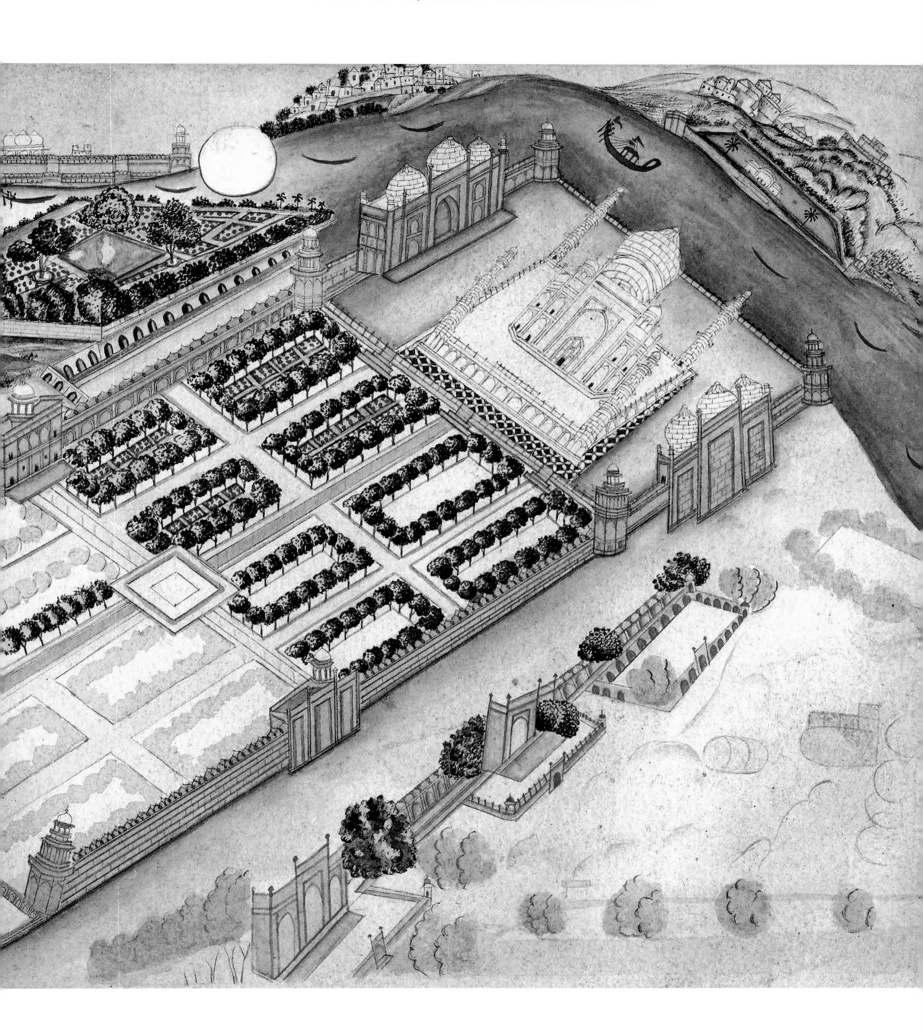

Left and below: The emperor's entrance is clearly visible in this 1937 photograph of the Taj Mahal from the riverside. Solid marble steps lead to a small door perhaps showcasing the humility of entering a sacred space, even though the north wall is elaborately embellished with carving and marble inlay for the emperor's viewing. The remaining walls enclosing the garden are austere and extremely high.

At this level, the graves were approached through galleries and suites that were accessible from the river. These rooms were elaborately painted with decorations befitting the royals. Now locked and, in some cases, bricked up, these spaces were exclusive to the emperor and his immediate family.

Certainly for Shah Jahan, this was to be his most visionary plan at a scale never seen before or since, and to execute it, craftsmen, calligraphers, draftsmen, all began to congregate in Agra. Contemporary records are clear that Ustad Ahmed Lahauri was Minar-i-Kul – Chief Architect – and his grave in Aurangabad records his distinctions as having completed the Taj Mahal in Agra and the Fort and Jama Masjid in Delhi. His son, Lutf Allah, wrote in the *Diwan-i-Muhandis*: 'Ahmad the architect *(mi'mar)* who in his art was a hundred steps ahead of the masters of this art, conversant with Euclid and his discourses and acquainted with all their particulars, the

mysteries of the planets and stars had become known to him, the mysteries of *Almagest* (Ptolemy's AD 150 study of Astronomy) had been understood by him.'[13] The entire complex is built on grids of the Mughal *gaz*, perhaps closest to the yard in scale while the grid provides classical order with flexibility within, and it is this which makes the complex seem so harmonious. Although the construction of the entire Taj Mahal complex took 22 years to complete, in 12 years, Lahauri records, the mausoleum was finished, which in itself was a mammoth enterprise. Reports on the progress of the work are limited, and while royal chronicles were written during the *urs*, few had construction details of this heavenly enterprise.

Bilateral symmetry or duality is at its apogée in the grand plan of the Taj Mahal, the importance of counterparts symbolising the intellectual and spiritual notions of harmony. Such symmetry and geometrical planning reflect Sura 36, no 36:

Glory to Allah who created
in pairs all things that
the earth produces, as well as
their own kind
And other things of which
they have no knowledge.[14]

Left, top: The Taj Mahal was designed to be accessed by Shah Jahan and the royal family who only ever approached the mausoleum by barge from the river. His vision therefore was circumscribed by this approach and their visit would have been limited to salutations at the grave. The perspective from the river, or indeed from anywhere, was designed so that no one could actually ever see the mausoleum in its entirety but rather in fragments, an essential design intention completely lost today.

Left and below: Today, the fresh-flowing waters of the River Yamuna have become a distant dream but the relationship to the river remains a constant reminder of the majesty of the design. Shah Jahan's arrival by boat at the Taj is also an imagination as the river now flows significantly higher and access to the monument from the river's edge is no longer possible.

Below: The Taj Mahal was built in perfect symmetry and alignment within the mausoleum and also the entire site. The mausoleum with the central walkway is the reality of today's imagination of the Taj as indeed it was for the common man who would visit the Taj to pay obeisance to the emperor. The wide central walkway on either side of the water channels is the perfect access but undoubtedly in Shah Jahan's life, it was limited to the privileged few as the public was largely restricted to outer chambers, for a mere glimpse of the mausoleum.

Every building in the Taj Mahal complex has a counterpart. Only the mausoleum stands alone and it is the pairing of buildings on either side of the central concourse with the tomb at the end, which underscores the allegory of duality in the planning as well as perfect balance. Similarly, the use of red sandstone and marble reflects the established order also seen in the plan and layout; red sandstone was, in effect, the image of the imperial Akbari buildings, symbolic of imperial supremacy, while white marble marks the transition of the spiritual and temporal, a precedent of representation, established by Shah Jahan in the Agra Fort. This is best expressed in the Taj Mahal with the marble edifice framed in buildings of red sandstone.

The lower platform is entirely in red sandstone, some thousand feet across and defined by two solid *burjs* at its four corners, with a mosque to the right of the mausoleum and the *Mehman Khana* or *Jawab* to the left. Together, they

provide the perfect foil to the towering, yet ethereal mausoleum. The extraordinary feature of this platform is that it is not solid but its weight is broken by passages and underground chambers. It is through these passages that Mumtaz Mahal's body was brought to its resting place, while later, Shah Jahan's body was brought by river from Agra Fort.

The mosque is a tripartite plan matched in the *Jawab* and is classical Shahjahani, in that, it is a long hall with three domes, the outer ones being smaller. The *Jamaat Khana* or *Jawab*, possibly meaning 'reflection', balances the symmetry of the composition and was originally used for important visitors, hence the *Mehman Khana*. It differs from the mosque only in that it lacks a *mihrab*. The entire expanse of the terrace has geometric-patterned flooring in red sandstone and marble, marking the beginning of the transition of pure and sacred space. This also established the hierarchy or protocol to attend the Taj with regard to who accessed which part of the complex – the royal family, the *ulema* and the *hafiz* would enter the sacred chambers, while below, yet much higher than the ground level was the congregation area for nobility and favoured followers who would not access the mausoleum.

At the centre of the *takht* or *kursi*, the mausoleum is the focus of an immense marble platform articulated with a minaret at each corner. These are some 43-metres high and were originally working minarets for the muezzin's call to prayer. The four minarets here are less functional and were used mainly to provide scale and proportion to the whole. The soaring white marble towers are broken by balconies, accessed through an internal staircase with small *chhattris* at the top level, and provide architectural balance and proportion for the central tomb. The minarets tilt ever so slightly outward, one school of thought being that if they fell during an earthquake, they would fall outward, but it was more likely to provide a perfect line of sight in terms of their immense height. They were described then 'like ladders reaching heavenwards.'[15] Minarets at four corners were already a feature in the Char Minar built in 1591, in the new city of Hyderabad, and were also used as much for call to prayer as to achieve architectural distinction.

The centrepiece is the mausoleum, a square building with chamfered corners, a complex of eight rooms clustered round the inner sepulchral space and based on the *hasht bihisht* principle described in the Quran, with the central room as its core. Defined by Lahauri as Baghdadi in plan, it is built at two immense levels, and the central space is separated from the outer rooms with

The use of red sandstone and marble came to charcterise the architecture of Shah Jahan in Agra. The red sandstone mosque (above) and the Mehman Khana (top) flank the pristine white mausoleum; the Shahjahani architectural vocabulary established by Shah Jahan in the Agra Fort but which reaches its apogee in the Taj Mahal, as the red sandstone buildings appear to provide the perfect frame for the pure marble edifice.

This and facing page: The massive brick structure encased in marble drew artisans and craftsmen from across India in what was at the time an industrial undertaking. Each flower was exquisitely carved and considering the profusion of carving, its perfection lies in the fact that it is never seen in excess. The balance of building mass and fine detail is immensely sophisticated at the Taj Mahal.

square latticed screens which provide an element of privacy as well as mystery to the cenotaphs. The outer chambers at the lower level are far more detailed than at the upper level, even though both are rendered in fine lime plaster finish. Notably, only the central royal chamber is in embellished marble where the emperor would have prayed, while the eight rooms which surround it were used by nobility and the *ulema*. The *hafiz* recited his prayers from here, their simplicity reflecting their devotional intent for which the acoustics of these chambers are remarkable, as the prayers resonated through the entire building.

The mausoleum is a massive brick structure with its walls several metres thick. On the outside, the façade is defined by two tiers of arched recesses, with a central *pishtaq* articulating the entrances on all four sides, each of which is detailed out almost identically. The *pishtaqs* are framed by panels of calligraphic inscriptions by Ammanat Khan of Shiraz, at an immense height over the arches. The calligraphy surrounding each portal is as wondrous in content as in execution. It is estimated that some 100 metres of inscriptions from the Quran are inlaid here – about Judgement Day and *jannat* – for the faithful. Ammanat Khan engraved his name and the date in the panels, which indicates that within four years, the building was in an advanced state of construction, inside and outside. When he completed the task, he was rewarded by Shah Jahan with an elephant and a higher rank. The calligraphy over the south *pishtaq* ushers the visitor into the sacred space: 'But O thou Soul rest in peace, Return

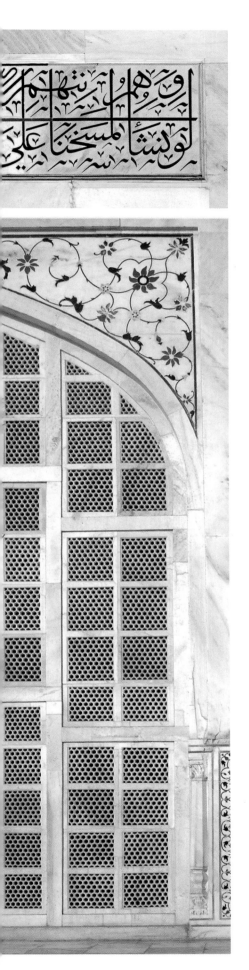

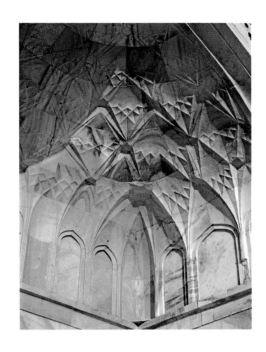

thou unto thy Lord well pleased and well pleasing unto him, Enter thou among my servants, And enter thou my paradise.'[16]

Equally, the frame of the arches are delicately inlaid in arabesques and scrolls, almost resembling European lyres, spilling out of the corners and connected by the finest tracery, its jewels glimmering in different lights of the day or seasons. Each element is perfect in design and rendition, the mass of the structure offset by the delicacy of its detailing. As one circumnavigates the outside of the mausoleum, the north-west corner barely conceals its secret – one lower supporting pillar is infinitesimally different. Whether the imperfection is embedded in the structure by the hand of the craftsman or the emperor is not known but it introduces an element of humility that only God is perfect, the flaw on the side facing the mosque being conceivably corroboration. Flaw and opinion, as known and practised in Islam, recognise that only God is perfect. Such flaws are often seen in carpets and other forms of craftsmanship as a token of humility where even the master craftsmen does not challenge the perfection achievable only by God.

The pinnacle of Mughal architecture and indeed of the era, was the dome of the Taj Mahal. It was, and remains, one of the world's highest domes as also, perhaps, the most elegant. The double dome had already been used by the Sultanate kings and so was not unknown but in the Taj Mahal, it rose to exceptional heights.

However, the centrepiece of the whole is the sepulchral chamber and nothing impinges on its perfection of design, scale or proportion. The central chamber exemplifies every aspiration of royal decree and ambition. It is octagonal; on four sides are huge arches in alignment with the *pishtaq* and designed for light, while the roof soars 'heavenwards'. It is entirely dressed in marble, and every surface finish is replete with meaning, design and allegory. Mumtaz Mahal's cenotaph is central to the entire space while Shah Jahan, who was buried later, is 'off-centre' but is, as expected, the much larger tomb of the two.

Such adornment was exclusively reserved for the royal family and in the Taj Mahal achieves immense symbology. The stylised jewelled inlay of iris, narcissus and tulips on the interior surfaces of the central chamber are for either the beloved or afterlife. The wall panels in *bas relief* have *guldastas* full of flowers while on the exterior surfaces of the tomb are similar designs but without the sophistication of the vases. The cenotaphs are screened by marble cutwork *jalis* of great refinement, and are also octagonal, in keeping with the *hasht bihisht* plan. It is richly embellished

Below: Even so there are infinitesimal imperfections worked into the building, small deviations embedded in the structure, as only God could be perfect.

Above and facing page: The mausoleum inside is splendidly executed. Rich in detail and perfect in execution, the interior is almost overwhelming in its design. The octagonal carved marble screen further extends the principles of the hasht bahisht *while the grave of Mumtaz Mahal is in perfect alignment with the northern* pishtaq. *The minute detail within is a contrast to the massive scale of the building itself.*

with *parchin kari* floral patterns. Together with the cenotaphs, the ensemble attains unsurpassable superiority in design and execution, with a richness and intensity never seen before. In the Illumined Tomb, Mughal architectural aspirations and their symbolism reached their zenith. The complex was conceivably viewed as a 'construct' of *jannat* on earth. In the Quran, those who are conscious of Allah are promised the parable of *jannat*, an unknown or mythical place, through which running waters flow but unlike an earthly garden, its fruits would be everlasting as would its shade. It is possible that *jannat* is envisioned here with its immense scale, proportions, decorations, geometry and everlasting flowers. The monument evokes a stylised garden of paradise, with floral patterns so prolific and fantastical that they could not be of this earth; the central chamber soaring 'heavenwards' is also conceived as a construct of *jannat*. 'And above this inner dome, radiant like the hearts of angels, has been raised another heaven-touching, guava-shaped *(amrudi-*

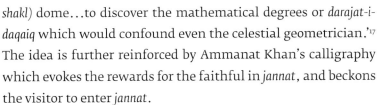

shakl) dome…to discover the mathematical degrees or *darajat-i-daqaiq* which would confound even the celestial geometrician.'[17] The idea is further reinforced by Ammanat Khan's calligraphy which evokes the rewards for the faithful in *jannat*, and beckons the visitor to enter *jannat*.

The tombs of the emperor and his wife are also quite different. Mumtaz's grave is embellished with Mughal floral patterns at its base and its elevated sepulchre, while flowery arabesque patterns render a rich surface, facing downwards in mourning. Quranic verses at the upper level further reinforce the prospect of *jannat*. At the foot of the grave, her epitaph is simple – 'The Illumined Tomb of Arjumand Banu Begum titled Mumtaz Mahal died in 1040' (AD 1631).

Shah Jahan's estranged son Aurangzeb provided him a grave which was significantly larger but not dignified with Quranic verse. His epitaph reads: 'This is the sacred grave of His Most Exalted Majesty, Dweller in Eternity, Second Lord of

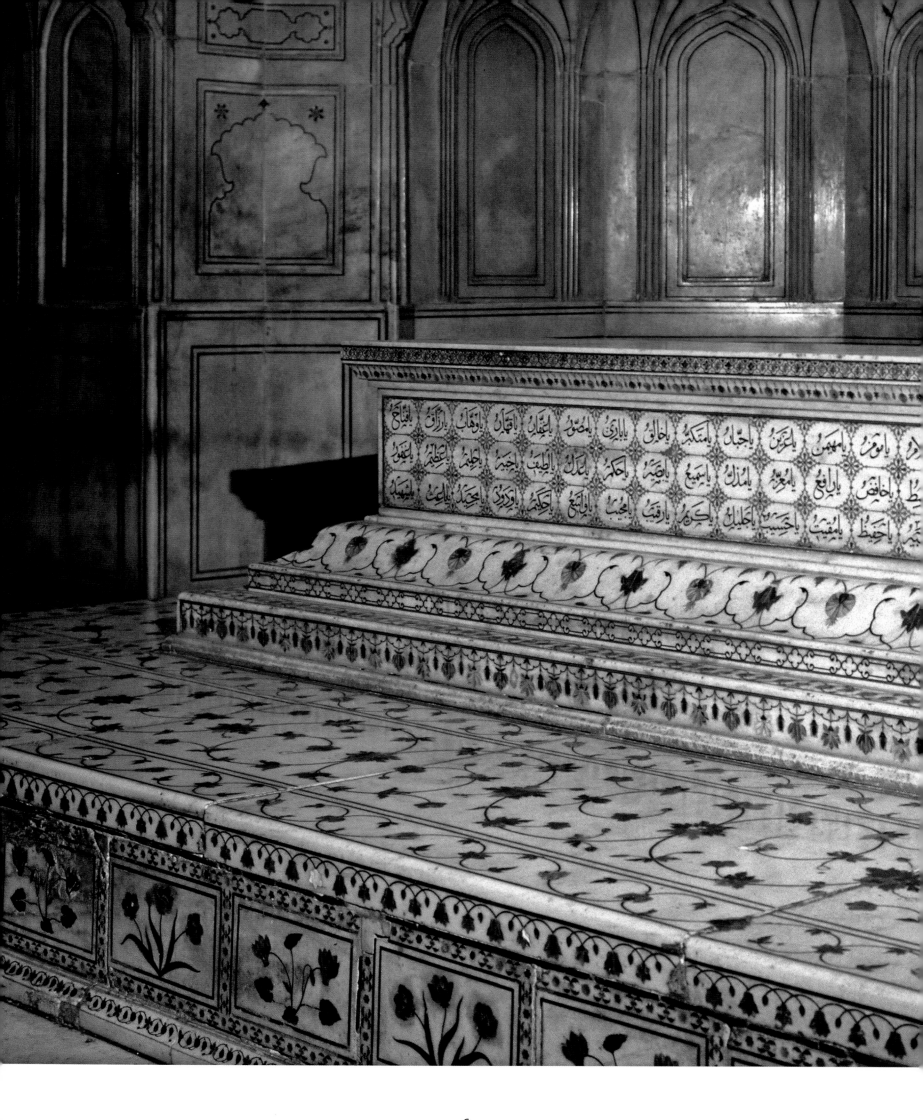

Left: The pristine Makrana marble mausoleum towers above the entire complex. It is defined by the details seen in its exquisite carvings, lattice jalis and spectacular squinched archways which have all been given equal attention to detail. The calligraphic inscriptions by Ammanat Khan of Shiraz, at the exaggerated height over the arches, are yet a wonder in design and execution. It is estimated that some 100 metres of inscriptions from the Quran are inlaid around the four entrances to the mausoleum.

Right: Mumtaz Mahal's grave has exceptional calligraphy, with the ninety-nine names of Allah inscribed over it, while Shah Jahan's grave, commissioned by Aurangzeb, is not so nuanced. It is exceptionally inlaid but no longer sacred.

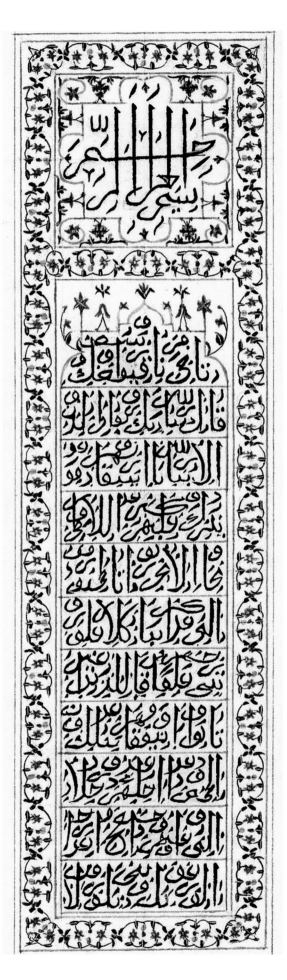

Far right: The stylised jewelled inlay of iris, narcissus and tulips on the interior surfaces of the central chamber are for either the beloved or the afterlife. The wall panels in bas relief have guldastas full of flowers and on the exterior surfaces of the tomb there are similar designs but without the sophistication of guldastas. The cenotaphs are screened by marble cutwork screens, heavily decorated and inlaid. This too is octagonal. Together, the ensemble attains heights of superiority in design and execution with a richness and intensity never seen before.

the Auspicious Conjunction, Shah Jahan Padshah; may it ever be fragrant. The year 1076' (1666 AD).

Below the cenotaphs, the austere marble crypt is accessed by a steep staircase and has the graves of the emperor and his wife in the same alignment as above, to ensure no one would walk over their tombs. Both graves are in a north-south alignment and the bodies inside would have been laid to rest facing Mecca. The merits of the emperor and his wife are engraved with eulogies worthy of their position.

Shah Jahan's grave is larger and much more elaborate, with a plinth and tombstone befitting his stature as Emperor of the World but without any Quranic text; it was royal but not sacred. Mumtaz Mahal's grave on a low platform is relatively simpler, but the grave has 90 names of Allah from the Quran, expressing His multiple attributes in exquisite and fine calligraphy. Shah Jahan would have commissioned Mumtaz Mahal's gravestone. Thus, patterns and concept are as sacred as the entire composition. Each element in the two chambers is detailed to such perfection and with such brilliance that the jewelled flowers which survived centuries of pillage that followed the collapse of the Mughal Empire, are so exceptional that their luminescence demonstrates the mastery in this skill. François Bernier who visited the Taj Mahal described it vividly but was careful to point out that though the small chamber under the dome was opened with much ceremony once a year (probably during the *urs*) no Christian was permitted to enter lest its sanctity be profaned.

Left and above: Of the flowers inlaid in the carved screen, it is said some have as many as a hundred pieces of inlay; these are not always authentic but considered allegorical, underscoring the idea that the floral and natural patterns used were often in the realm of the imagination. The original inlays, especially of the floral patterns, were in deep-cut precious and semi-precious stones, intensely detailed but both prolific and fantastical.

THE SACRED AND SECULAR

The south wall opposite the tomb at the far end of the *char bagh* is more elaborate as it is double arcaded and so used by visitors who couldn't access the main tomb, yet they could still see *jannat* as Shah Jahan desired – from a public-viewing arcade. It is a huge arcaded platform, so that at no point is the view of the Taj Mahal ever obscured, defined by the two strong towers similar to the ones flanking the main platform, ensuring that the counterpart structures maintain the balance throughout the complex. At the centre of this wall is the great gate which 'raises its head to the sky'[18] announcing to all, *jannat* is within.

Gates in Mughal buildings were designed as symbols of power. The Buland Darwaza at Fatehpur Sikri demonstrates Mughal power at its zenith. Even the entrance to Akbar's tomb at Sikandra was built on a stupendous scale. At the Taj Mahal, notionally, the gate is the threshold between the earthly world and the aspiration inside. Even this is in the classic octagonal plan while the central space too has a very high ceiling, its arched entrance marking that point of transition. There is

This and facing page: Surrounding the Taj Mahal are almost equally handsome buildings. They were built for every possible need to make the complex self-sufficient. The burjs flanking the mosque and the Jawab have baolis as well as toilets. The khwasspuras housed servants or staff and this too was an independent space, not unlike a serai, while shops lined the Jilau Khana catering to the endless stream of visitors. The red sandstone was carved, plasters were painted but the rhythm of the dominance of the red with details of white creates a distinctive architectural vocabulary. The remarkable feature is the perfect symmetry of these structures on either side of the mausoleum and along its entire length. The mausoleum in white marble located within the red sandstone attains immense significance in its entirety.

no central dome but many cupolas on its arcaded roof seem to corroborate the charming legend that they represent the years it took to build the Taj Mahal.

The hierarchy of Shah Jahan's grand plan becomes clear as one moves away from the mausoleum complex. Beyond the immense gateway, the plans maintain the same order in layout but the adornment is absent. It was no longer a royal precinct: the ground of the *Jilau Khana* was unpaved; it was rough and unfinished and at a lower level. The *Jilau Khana* was intended to be an immense space where visitors could foregather, and perhaps even glimpse the mausoleum, its true glory visible only to the chosen few. It served as an intermediary space, the filter between the sacred and the profane. Riders, carriages and attendants would dismount and congregate here, a place to pause before moving towards the heavenly entity.

The *Jilau Khana* is entered through the gates in the eastern and western walls and the pathway to the gate is also flanked by arcaded corridors with bazaars that provided for visitors. Behind the bazaar walls, on either side and in continuation of the southern wall of the main complex, are the *khwasspuras* where the attendants of the tombs stayed. These are *serais* with small living spaces around a courtyard with a toilet block at the far end. The *khwasspuras*, and the *hafiz* who prayed at the tomb and were devoted to the services of the departed, remained here for many generations.

The fourth gate of the *Jilau Khana* is to the south and is known as Sidhi Darwaza. A simpler gate, it is reached up a flight of stairs leading to Charsu Bazaar, or Taj Ganj, as it is

known today; it marks the transition from the ruler to the ruled. The bazaar was designed to be the economic engine for the Taj Mahal. It has the same footprint as the rest of the complex and is set in four quadrants, with a *serai* in each quadrant. Together, these open onto an octagonal courtyard at the centre, the melting pot of all who ever visited. The first two *serai*s adjacent to the gate were built by the emperor and had 136 rooms, each with courtyards at the centre.

The *serai*s were built for merchants and traders who would bring jewels, velvets and other fineries to not only sell to visitors to the Taj Mahal, but also as furnishings for the Taj. All manner of goods and services could be obtained in Taj Ganj. An idea of what sort of goods might have been traded is found in the names for the *caravanserai*s – the northwestern one was known as Katra Omar Khan or Market of Omar Khan; the northeastern was called Katra Fulel or the Perfume Market; Katra Resham provided silk and Katra Jogidas was yet another merchant. Trade flourished and, in time, the merchants built their houses beyond Taj Ganj, extending the reach of this very formal, planned city. Gradually, the area expanded to provide for the needs of the workforce as well as the trade which generated revenues for the upkeep of the Taj Mahal.

The clear distinction between the sacred part of the complex and the secular is best seen here. Whilst the rest of the complex was funded by the *waqf* set up for its maintenance, Taj Ganj was left to its own devices to grow and survive as best it could. The contrast between the Taj Mahal's formal layout, supported by 30 revenue villages dedicated to it, and the narrow streets with organic constructions in Taj Ganj, is stark. On the 12th Urz marking the official end of the construction, rent money from the entire bazaar was acquired in perpetuity, yielding an income of two lakh rupees a year. No longer useful, Taj Ganj became *waqf* property with the imperial minister, eunuch Agah Khan, in charge. Tavernier's records of the time described it as 'a large bazaar consisting of six larger courts, all surrounded with porticos under which are the chambers of the merchants and an enormous quantity of cotton is sold here.'[19] It was a huge food market and Peter Mundy records the availability of beef, mutton, partridge, quails, turtle doves, mangoes, plantains and pineapples. It was also a large market for dried fruit.

Today, only fragments of the original constructions remain, most notably, the gates. The rest has been absorbed seamlessly into the bustling urbanisation which engulfed Agra.

Above and facing page, bottom: Agra had an abundance of world-renowned bazaars. These bazaars once known as 'the emporium of the traffic of the world' were global marketplaces. Often streets or areas were named after particular skills or trade. Great swathes of thatch protected the buildings from the intense summer heat.

Facing page top: The grander mansions of the rich merchants in Agra, often situated along the river, sometime accommodated shops on the street side but were generally introverted in nature and organised around courtyards which were entered through a well defined entrance gateway.

Following pages: The Taj Mahal undoubtedly is one of the most photogenic buildings in the world. While symmetrically proportioned when viewed frontally, it allows for varied visual compositions and juxtapositions of its elements, depending on the vantage point of the viewer. frontally, it allows for multiple visual compositions of its elements, depending on the position of the viewer.

3
Crafting the Taj

The Taj Mahal is perfectly clad in milk white Makrana marble, perhaps the device with which the building attains its sense of weightlessness and ephemeral quality. This move, besides resonating powerfully the sense of purity and the related deeper political symbolism, makes the building architecturally unique and visually powerful in terms of its presence on the landscape. The underlying structure of the Taj Mahal is one of masonry – massive brick walls modulated structurally to bear the immense thrust of the double domes that give it the visually perfect profile. This underlying masonry structure is then clad, like a skin over a body, taut, like cloth stretched over the bones of the building, evoking a lightness and luminosity which at the time perhaps no other building of this scale had achieved.

Makrana marble was the finest stone in Hindustan. Makrana lies some 300 kms west of Agra, and in an arrangement with Raja Jai Singh, the marble of this particular region was not only committed but delivered to Shah Jahan. Makrana marble is milky white and the highest quality is not opaque but slightly translucent, which gives it an ethereal quality – luminescent by day and night – as it dramatically alters its appearance in different lights. This luminescence had a particular resonance with Mughal sensibilities according to which light falling on the tomb had a metaphoric meaning associated with the presence of God.

Transporting the marble was an industry in itself as thousands of tonnes of immense marble slabs were moved by bullock carts from the quarries to the site, across the plains of Hindustan for the making of the Taj Mahal. Speaking of the size of this enterprise, Manrique Sebastian's records in 1641 state that the marble slabs

Facing page: The massive structure of the Taj Mahal is a perfect balance of monumental scale and more human dimensions can be seen between the mass of the dome and the relatively small entrance stairway – a sensitivity evident throughout the monument.

being transported were '...of such unusual size and length that they drew the sweat of many powerful teams of oxen and of the fierce-looking big-horned buffaloes which were dragging enormous...wagons in teams of twenty or thirty animals.'[1] Acquisition of marble was done by royal decree and no effort or cost was spared to acquire the best marble in all of Hindustan. Equally, there was to be no shortfall and no problem that could not be surmounted. The emperor's *firmans* were clear and addressed Raja Jai Singh as early as September 1632 that he should know 'Mulkshah has been deputed to Amber (Amer) to bring marble from the new mines (of Makrana). It is commended that carts on hire be arranged for transportation of marble and Mulkshah be assisted to purchase as much marble as he may desire to have. The purchase price of marble and cartage shall be paid by him from the treasury. Every other assistance be given to him to procure and bring marble and sculptors to the capital expeditiously.'[2]

By February 1633, the procurement was at its zenith as is clear in the emperor's next *firman*: 'As a great number of carts are required for transportation of marble needed for constructing building (at the capital), a *firman* was previously sent to you (to procure them). This is again desired of you, that as many carts on hire be arranged as possible in the earliest time, as has already been written to you, and be dispatched to Makrana for expediting the transport of marble to the capital. Every assistance be given to Ilahdad who has been deputed to arrange the transportation of marble to Akbarabad. Account (of expenditure on carts) along with the previous account of amount allocated for the purchase of marble be submitted (to the *mutsaddi* in charge of payment).'[3]

Five years on, problems of procurement persisted and the emperor's demands were by now almost unreasonable as clearly all resources were to remain focussed on his single project. According to his orders dated 7 Saffer, 1047 Al Hijra (June 21, 1637), 'We hear that your men detain the stone-cutters of the region at Amber and Rajnagar. This creates shortage of stone-cutters (miners) at Makrana and the work (of procuring marble) suffers. Hence, it is desired of you that no stone-cutter be detained at Amber and Rajnagar and all of them who are available be sent to the *mutsaddis* of Makrana.'[4]

Naturally in the sequence of things, to secure the imagined edifice on the fluid and unstable river bank, the first component of the building was the foundation. An interesting record of the conception of the foundations is provided by Mr. H.I.S. Kanwar, an ASI officer-writer, who in 1972 wrote: 'It is calculated that in the first week of December 1631, that is sometime before prince Shah Shuja's departure with his mother's coffin from Burhanpur, the levelling work on the site would have been completed satisfactorily. Immediately thereafter, the engineers busied themselves with the next important task, namely, the provision of a strong foundation stout enough to withstand the heavy structure weighing lakhs of tons, comprising the platform and mausoleum clothed in marble, and the mosque to its west and the latter's complement to its east, both in red sandstone. [...] Since the northern perimeter of the great basin lies along the riverbank, some facts about Jamuna may not be out of place. The banks of the river are generally hard and stable, and scored by numerous ravines. The breadth of the stream varies from 500 feet to a quarter of a mile. The depth is nowhere very great, and even in rains it seldom exceeds ten feet. At Agra,

Facing page: Marble quarried from what remains till today India's finest marble mines, was sourced at a great distance from Agra in Makrana, Rajasthan. Today, while hauling and transportation may be mechanised, the mines are larger than ever and quarried at great depth to source the purest milky white marble, still much coveted.

Below: The immense doorways of the monument are in perfect proportion with the scale of the entire building; the calligraphy too is perfectly executed, the human form miniscule in this ambition.

it averages eight feet when full and only two feet in the dry weather, though in exceptional floods, the water reaches a height of nearly 29 feet. Its velocity has been estimated at two miles an hour in the normal season but during the rains, it has been known to attain a speed of seven-and-a-half miles (an hour). Over 200 years ago, except for a couple of canals dug north of Delhi by Firoz Shah Tughlaq in the latter half of the 14th century, there were hardly any canals in the Agra region to divert the vast volume of water, and thus the Jamuna stream was broader and deeper. It is estimated that in 1631-32, this stream extended over half a mile during the rains, decreasing to about 450 yards in the dry season, and its depth varied between 25 and 12 feet respectively. Our contention is based on the premise that, as the capital of the Moghal Empire, Agra was a focus of river traffic. This, in turn, is evident from a 150-year-old painting which depicts the presence of fairly large boats plying on the Jamuna River past the northern perimeter wall of the Taj Mahal, and also shows the existence of two openings in this wall to allow entry from the riverside (into the subterranean chambers under the mausoleum), the water level of the stream being just below these openings and about 37 feet below garden level. The position of these openings must have been fixed above the observed maximum level of the stream.'⁵

The foundation, or literally the base of the Taj Mahal, was not a conventional one but conceived as a series of structures that could also respond to the fluctuating level of the dynamic river. Mr. H.I.S. Kanwar describes the genius of the foundation structure: 'The foundation area, what is known today as the Great Basement, was conveniently divided into three parts, namely, one on which the mausoleum was to be erected comprising nearly one-third (313 feet square), and the remaining two extending equally on either side of the central one. The mausoleum site was dug in the form of wells about 44-feet deep and spaced out at suitable intervals. Their diameter varying between 10 and 15 feet, these wells were mainly concentrated under the mausoleum plinth area (186 feet x 186 feet) where they numbered about 30. A larger number dug along the northern perimeter of the Great Basement, were arranged in series of seventeen, seven and three, in order to allow for a compact foundation, strong enough to counteract river erosion. The bottom of these wells was filled with rubble masonry mixed with hydraulic lime, its estimated height being two-and-a-half feet, above which poles of sal wood 8 to 10 inches

Left: A charming 19th-century drawing of the Taj shows just how difficult it was to replicate the perfection of the monument. Its delicate and detailed embellishments were as complicated to draw and many similar images of the time were picturesque but hardly accurate.

This drawing is of special interest as it depicts a waterway and the relation of the river to the monument at least 150 years ago.

Left: Today, the riverfront has transformed. It is no longer navigable but more critically, the river no longer flows along the edge of the mausoleum. This has raised serious concerns that the foundations of the Taj Mahal are no longer as stable given the change in the water table. On the contrary, studies have shown that the foundations of the Taj Mahal are absolutely sound and weathering the changes remarkably well.

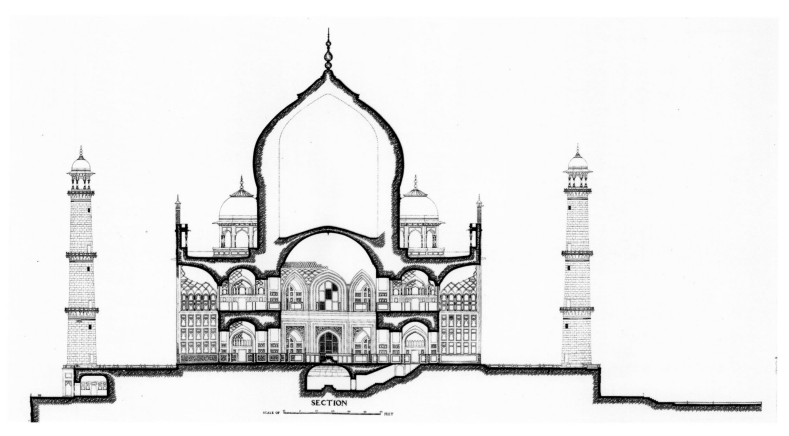

SECTION

SCALE OF   FEET

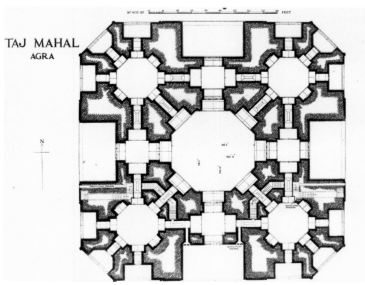

TAJ MAHAL
AGRA

N

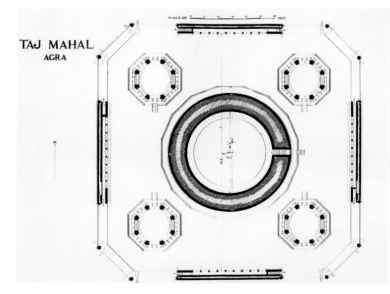

TAJ MAHAL
AGRA

N

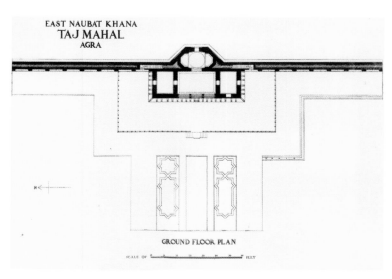

EAST NAUBAT KHANA
TAJ MAHAL
AGRA

N

GROUND FLOOR PLAN

SCALE OF   FEET

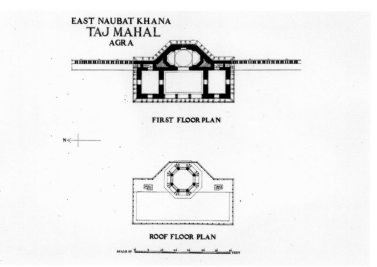

EAST NAUBAT KHANA
TAJ MAHAL
AGRA

FIRST FLOOR PLAN

N

ROOF FLOOR PLAN

SCALE OF   FEET

Preceding pages: The Taj Mahal is one of the most intensely documented buildings in India. These 19th-century drawings capture the scale, height and majesty of the interior more than an authentic rendering.

in diameter and around 40-feet tall were piled upright atop the above-stated masonry resting securely on the bedrock below. These poles were joined together in groups of about nine each, with iron bands riveted with copper bolts, and axels at intervals to hold the poles in place. These facts about the foundation's structure were confirmed in the latter half of 1958 during a chance investigation by the ASI, made in regard to a suspected depression on one side of the Great Basement. The sal wood was brought from Terel forests in what is known today as Uttar Pradesh, probably because it was nearest to Agra, for it is well known that sal wood is also available in Madhya Pradesh. [...] What was the reason for the incorporation of upright wooden poles in the foundation system? Wood, being not as rigid (as would have been the case with the foundation made entirely of masonry) and, therefore, having a certain amount of flexibility, had the ability of absorbing the effect of earthquakes to which Agra was prone. The use of wood indicates that Shah Jahan's master builders were aware of the above-stated shock-bearing characteristics, and knew that in the event of an earthquake,

the superstructure would be limited to a sway but not rock. This may well account for the survival of the Taj Mahal of such danger during the past three-and-a-half centuries. Sal wood was selected for its several good qualities: it is a solid wood, known for its great strength and long durability; it has the inherent quality of long preservation, and in the open, it has the ability of preserving itself without seasoning or treatment without preservative. That the Moghul builders were aware of these qualities is evident from an ancient saying: *"Sau sal kharhi, sau sal parhi, sau sal garhi"*, meaning literally that it can outlast "a century standing, a century in lying position, (and) a century underground." Likewise, copper was incorporated for two main reasons: it acted as a preserver for both iron and wood against rust and deterioration, respectively, and among the base metals, copper stands alone in its resistance to soil corrosion. Copper, according to Abul Fazl, was mined in various parts of northern India, especially Rajputana, and was available in reasonable quantities, a situation persisting in the 17th century. The vacant space in each well and the rest of the gaping abyss was filled with a mixture of granite stone rubble and mortar. A chemical analysis of a sample of this mortar, carried out during repairs to the Taj Mahal in 1943 revealed that it was composed of 80% calcium carbonate, 78% clay, and the balance of 8% comprised iron organic impurities, magnesia, moisture and sulphate. It could be scratched with an ordinary pen-knife only with difficulty, and was found extremely hard, especially at the core. A sample piece kept under water showed no signs of softening, and instead, retained its original hardness and compactness. In order to ensure the correct orientation of the *mihrab* of the mosque on the west of the mausoleum, the northern perimeter of the Great Basement of the rectangle had to be aligned accurately in an east-west direction and, therefore, some portions of the riverbank falling within it had to be reclaimed for inclusion in the construction of the foundation, which was built up to a height of 4 feet above garden level.'[6]

As the foundations were completed and materials were to be hoisted for the upper levels, immense mud ramps were constructed and a huge number of oxen and even elephants were used to move materials, the scale of the ramp increasing with the building; it is speculated that these ramps were over two miles in length. Attention would have been paid to its embellishment with semi-precious jewels and fine stones procured from all over India and Asia. Red sandstone was

Left and bottom: In Agra, the Mughals had, since the time of Babur, built their riverfront gardens across the river from the city, in effect depriving the river of its flood plain. The foundations of the Taj Mahal have always been viewed as an engineering marvel as they are not just supporting the massive walls at the river edge to push back the Yamuna but also the foundation system for the entire mausoleum. To construct a building of this scale on the waterfront was no mean achievement, especially during the monsoons when the river rose to alarming heights. These well foundations which underpin the Taj Mahal had in fact been used along the entire waterfront on both sides of the river. As siltation has built up over time, many of the riverfront gardens now appear to be set back from the river, and an increasing number of well foundations are visible.

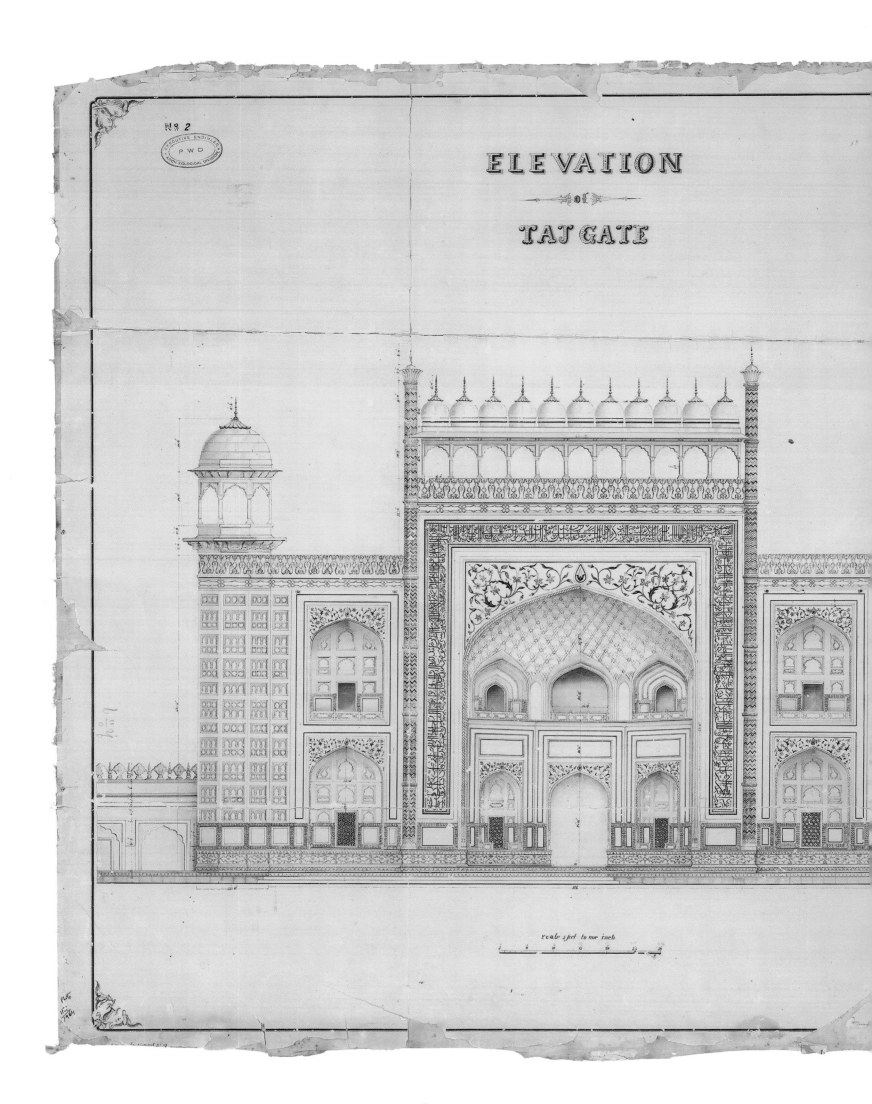

ELEVATION
of
TAJ GATE

scale 4 feet to one inch

TAJ GATE

WEST ELEVATION

These skillfully executed drawings of the main gate are an important archival record. The main gate is a large structure with great presence supported by four burjs which define its scale, and it also successfully screens the mausoleum from the public eye. The southern façade is capped with smaller cupolas apocryphally supposed to denote the number of years it took to build the Taj Mahal. There is no evidence of this theory but these cupolas do serve to lighten the building mass as they are built over small cupped arches. The calligraphy over the main archway beckons the public to "enter jannat". The west face is one which is rarely seen today as it is almost lost in the crowding of entry and exits but it showcases the detail and perfection achieved in each element – especially the gateway which effectively marks the transition between the sacred and the secular.

Following pages 158-165: In direct contrast to the huge scale of the building, the carvings and inlay inside the tomb achieve the acme of design and craftsmanship. Although the marble screen is a later addition, having replaced the gold screen, nonetheless it is superb in both carving and inlay. Each flower is an artwork by itself, each petal a masterpiece which when it was made would have had the brilliance of the jewels of Asia. Today, most of the inlay is replaced as the jewels were stolen after the fall of the Mughal Empire, but they are a mere shadow of what they would have been. Inside the mausoleum, much of the original inlay survived but it was around the tombs themselves that really fine inlay and carving is concentrated. These drawings are artworks in themselves as they faithfully recorded each detail of the decoration.

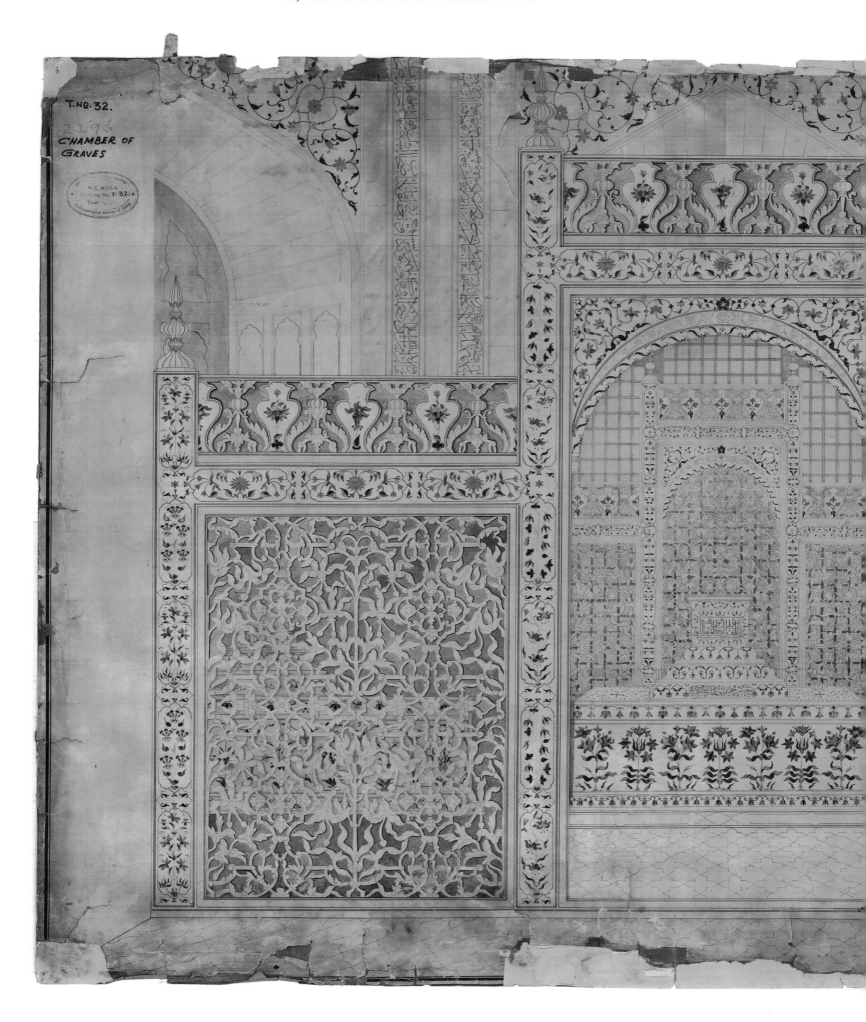

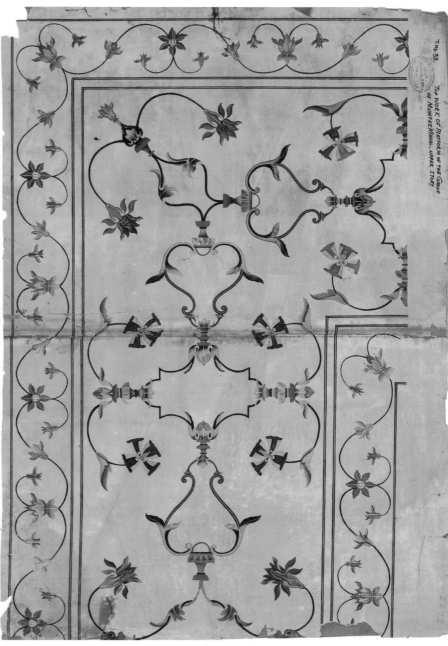

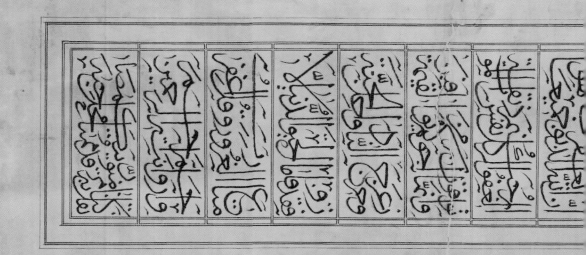

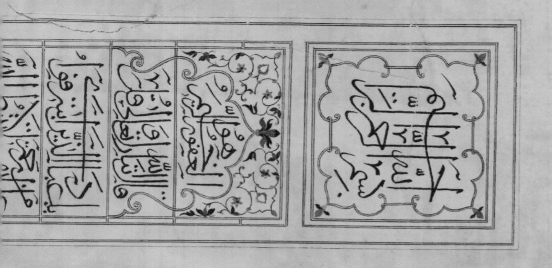

EAL GRAVE OF
SHAH JAHAN

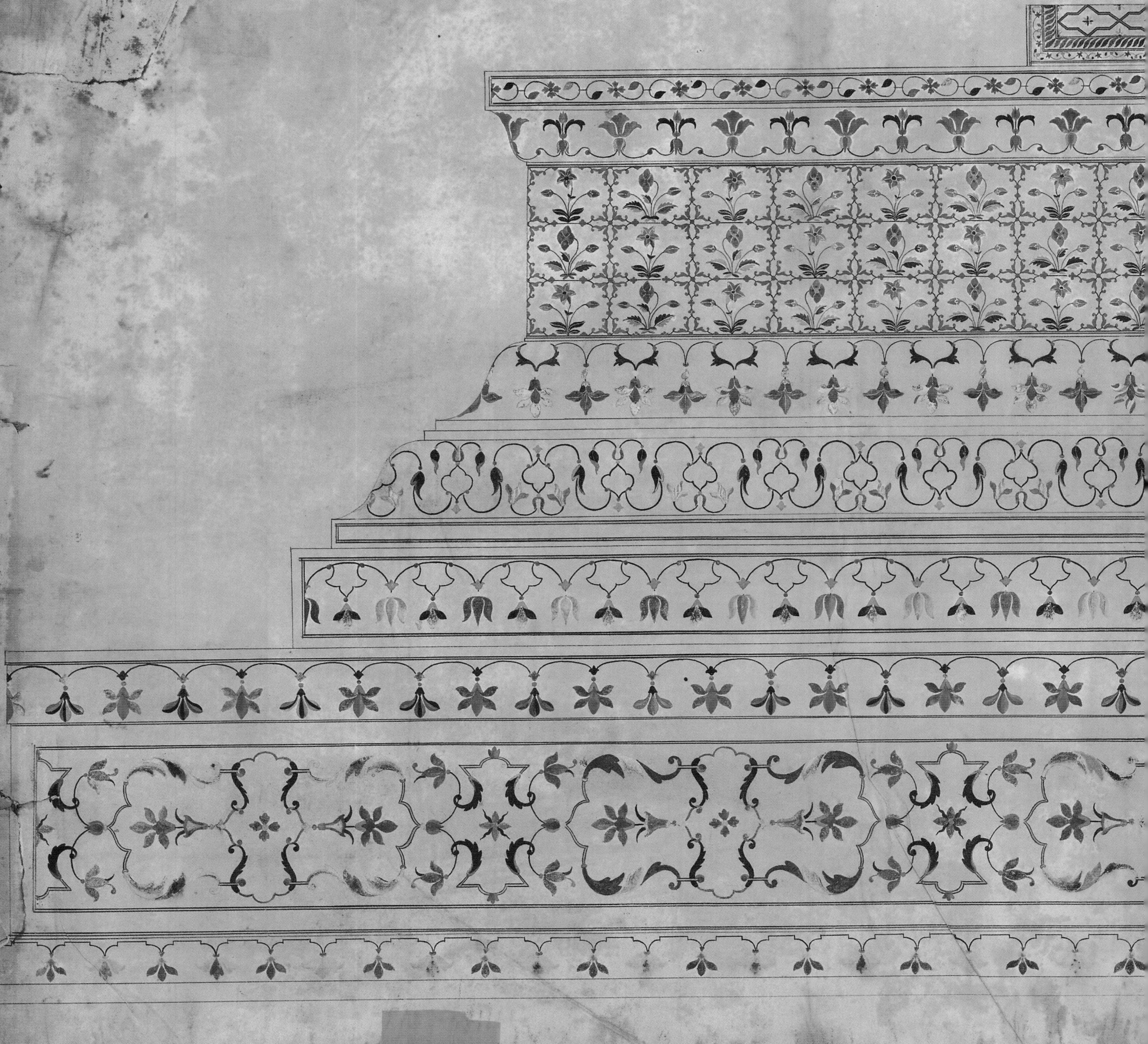

2295

from neighbouring Fatehpur Sikri, Tantpur and Paharpur, rare turquoise from distant Tibet, lapis lazuli from Afghanistan, sapphire from Ceylon and carnelian from Arabia. In all, 28 types of precious and semi-precious stones were inlaid into white marble.[7]

Naturally, in this construction process, the craftsmen were the crucial resource. In his descriptions of the Taj Mahal, Lahauri is aware of the scale if not the detail: 'And from all parts of the empire there are assembled great numbers of skilled stone-cutters, lapidaries and inlayers, each one an expert in his art, who commenced work along with other craftsmen...'[8] Master masons and their men were either commandeered or gravitated to Agra for what seemed secure employment. Marble craftsmen were distinct from sandstone craftsmen for each had a specialised skill.

Of particular interest are the markings on the stone, especially on the red sandstone flooring, used extensively in

Crafting the monument entailed creating a massive workforce. Craftsmen from across the country gravitated to Agra to serve at what would at any time be considered an industrial undertaking. Stone cutters, carvers, inlay workers built a mausoleum so fine that it has never been replicated. It is likely many went to Delhi to build Shah Jahan's new capital. Others stayed back and subsequent generations are still engaged in the craft, though on a far more modest scale.

Above: Major floods in 1922 transformed the landscape of the Agra waterfront, leaving behind a build-up of silt. Over successive years, the entire waterfront changed.

Right: Conservation of the Taj Mahal has been going on for over 150 years as both vandalism and age took their toll on the fabric of the monument.

India. These are seen in temples at Bhojpur, the Rajwada in Indore and at Itimad-ud-Daulah and Fatehpur Sikri. Popularly known as mason marks, there are over 425 such marks. Some are only symbols and others along the side of a stone are complete names. These names have been translated by the ASI and are an informative record of who worked at the Taj Mahal construction site. The symbols appear to be those of the contractor; his workforce being skilled but unlettered, each master mason would have had a symbol given to the stone-cutter to systematically account for the work done. At the very least then, there would have been over 400 contractors at the site, each with his team of stone-masons, with his own guild marks. They evoke the scale of work and activity at the site which was beyond the high masonry walls of the main complex and, therefore, unknown to the chroniclers of the court who wrote only of the munificence within. These marks, notable in the sandstone and not on

the marble, reflect the workforce that was engaged in the broader Taj Mahal complex, garden and surroundings.

The broader complex of the Taj Mahal is as important a spatial articulation as the building itself. Besides the many peripheral buildings that housed supporting services, just the perimeter walls were important architectural elements as they isolated and made precious through separation, the *jannat* within. The expanse of these perimeter walls and their construction also engaged a skilled workforce at a scale that merits attention. Mr H.I.S. Kanwar describes this lucidly: 'It is calculated that the construction of the perimeter wall commenced more or less immediately after the levelling of the site had been completed, and perhaps about the same time when the work of building the foundation had been taken up. The erection of this wall began simultaneously at the riverside ends of the western and eastern perimeter, where the angles of the foundation were adorned with lovely octagonal turrets. From the riverbank to the southern end of the garden is a distance of very nearly 1,500 feet, over which rose a well 19 feet 6 inches high and 6 feet 8 inches thick, as may be observed today. This latter dimension facilitated the task of the watch and ward because the guards could easily march up and down from their posts atop the wall. The heavy structure of such a high wall needed a strong foundation, and it is not surprising that it has a depth of around 5 feet below ground level. Leave alone the perimeter walls, as the core of the structure of the mausoleum and other components of the Taj Mahal complex was to be built in brick, a gargantuan amount was required and, therefore, a convenient source of material was desirable. This was found in the neighbourhood of the Taj Mahal site, where the clay was three-fifth silica in content and thus quite suitable for manufacture of bricks, all hand moulded. As the average size of the brick was 6.5 x 4.5 x 1.5 inches, a greater quantity of mortar had to be employed due to its small dimensions. Constructed in this manner, the core of the structure was extra strong, capable of long durability and withstanding the vicissitudes of the weather. With the building work in progress, it would not be difficult to visualise the vast multitude of diggers, bricklayers, labourers, masons and other artisans, who numbered thousands, in all twenty thousand, according to the French traveller Tavernier who visited Agra not very long afterwards.'[9]

As the main Taj Mahal grew in height, scaffolding was erected which was almost as dense as the structure itself. It is

Top: The frontage, or northern wall of the Taj Mahal completely silted up after the floods and gradually the emperor's entrance was obliterated.

Above: Conservation of many monuments of the period remain an ongoing challenge as the urban landscape alters irrevocably.

Below: Watercolours of the most visible monument of the fledging East India Company were in abundance. Some were classical drawings and serve as exemplary records of the time. Others such as this one assume more decorative and artistic imaginations.

often debated whether this was in traditional Indian bamboo or in bricks as some early records indicate. Brick-making kilns and marble artisans would have consumed the largest amount of land. The inlay preparation alone was a mammoth undertaking as jewels had to be reduced to infinitesimal sizes and inlaid at the height of the *pishtaq*; marble slabs were dressed and taken up huge ramps to be affixed. It was a monumental undertaking.

Over 20 years, more than 20,000 workers were engaged to build the mausoleum complex at a cost of five million rupees. Begley states that Shah Jahan's budget for buildings was

25 million rupees, and five million was 20 per cent of the entire building budget of Shah Jahan's empire. Shahjahanabad was already under construction, so clearly there were sufficient resources for the aggrandisement of the emperor. Shah Jahan spared no expense for the Taj Mahal. Grains were diverted to Agra to feed the workforce; workers had to be fed in order to complete his *jannat*. Lands around the Taj Mahal were made desolate while the mausoleum was being built; the vast workforce and their dependents were temporary settlers encamped in amongst what could arguably be described as an immense building site. While there are records of payments,

Following pages: The vaulted dome of the mausoleum showcases the immense height of the dome and the engineering skills it would have drawn on at the time to achieve this. The interior is inlaid and carved in as much detail in the dome as it is at the level of the pishtaq.

there is little record of how 20,000 workers were managed at a scale of operations uncharted before. Some particular names surface in records about the construction but these would have probably been the master craftsmen who supervised the crucial elements of the building. For example, Ammanat Khan was paid around Rs 1,000 a month as was Isa Shirazi, the architect. Today, this would be approximately Rs 5,00,000. Interestingly, the master mason, Muhammad Hanief, from Kandahar earned the same amount but Ismail Khan Rumi was clearly not a nobleman as he earned just half the amount for the immense responsibility of making one of the finest domes ever built. The inlay workers who earned Rs 400 each were from Kannauj and were Hindu while the flower carvers came from Bukhara. There are no records of the thousands of workers who would have inhabited the site, making bricks or chiselling stone. Or indeed, of the many who would have died in the course of creating the emperor's *jannat*.

A *waqf* was established for the perpetual upkeep of the mausoleum with an income of Rs 4,00,000 from the annual revenues of 30 villages of the dependence of the Caliphate

of Akbarabad and Nagarchain. Lahauri records that it was decided at that point that should the building need repair, it should be from the income of these endowments. One third of this income came from the revenue villages, while the remainder came from taxes generated as a result of trade from the bazaars and *caravanserais* of Taj Ganj. Any surplus would be distributed by the emperor as he deemed fit. Besides paying for routine maintenance, the *waqf* financed the expenses for the tomb attendants and the *hafiz*, who would sit day and night in the mausoleum, reciting prayers. In the continuous living traditions Hindustan is still renowned for, *khadims* of the Taj were hereditary positions and the last of the direct descendents was employed by the ASI late into the 20th century.

As the construction of the Taj Mahal neared completion and the scaffolding, its beauty and proportions were suddenly manifest in people's imagination and on the landscape. Finally revealed, the silhouette of the Taj Mahal would certainly have created an unprecedented visual impact. The dome, its lightness and ethereal quality implying the lightness of a white cloth stretched over the profile of the dome, must have stunned the viewer. Architecturally, the dome of the Taj Mahal is distinctive in that it rests on an elegant drum or neck, reducing its visual weight tremendously – it is believed, that this has been inspired by the human proportions of the head in relation to the neck. Gracing the elegant neck is a wreath of inlaid flowers, all facing down in perpetual mourning.

While much has been written and recorded of the mathematical precision of the design of the dome, barely visible are sketches of the dome carved with calculations notated 74.22 metres below on the floor of the *Jawab*. This raises the possibility that while the dome was still being built, perhaps the dome design was fine-tuned by sight and perspective correction as much as by clever mathematical calculation. One has only to imagine Ustad Lahauri with his *karigar* sitting on the floor of the *Jawab*, debating the exact curve for the dome as the notations and drawings on the floor seem to suggest. Nearby, the *farma* of the finial of the Taj embedded in the floor, was created by 19th-century restorers to ensure the newly fabricated finial was exact before it was replaced. Such remnants keep alive the process of crafting the Taj and the evolution of the subtly nuanced details.

At the top of the dome is an inverted lotus, a *kalash* and a finial – visibly indigenous elements of a now obvious syncretic culture are introduced here. According to Lahauri, the finial was once covered in gold and some 11-yards high,

Today, restoration work at the Taj Mahal still engages with skilled craftsmen, without doubt descendents of the original families who moved to Agra. The jewelled inlay, vandalised over time, is methodically restored, the lapis lazuli inlay perhaps no longer two inches but a few millimetres deep. The Taj Mahal always has craftsmen restoring some element of the building, either replacing missing or damaged marble inlay or flooring worn away with the heavy tourist footfalls seen today.

The extraordinary inlays in the Taj Mahal showcases the great craftsmanship prevalent in India then and today even though the scale and breadth of work has changed. Today, marble carving and inlay are well-known living traditions of Agra.

raising the overall height to 107 yards above ground level. Lahauri described his overall experience thus: 'All over the interior and exterior of this mausoleum, artisans creating wonders and magic designs have inlaid (*parchin kari*) carnelian and other kinds of coloured stones.'[10]

The Taj Mahal is full of details and nuances that are hard to fully capture. The richly conceived and elaborately decorated central chamber is designed to elevate the senses. The lapidary is often considered to be Italian in origin but its execution at the Taj is by Indian craftsmen. Even though François Bernier compared it with the *pietra dura* of the Grand Dukes' Chapel in Florence, there is little evidence that it was an inspiration. In its time, the tomb was furnished with rich Persian carpets, gold lamps and candlesticks. It is reported that two great silver doors to the entrance were looted and melted down by Suraj Mal in 1764, and earlier, in 1720, a *chaddar* of pearls covering the cenotaph was carried off by Amir Husein Ali Khan. These accounts are endless and perhaps speak about the intense engagement of the patron and his desire to create not only something perfect in its conception but one embodied with all the energy and richness that he could provide.

But all was not perfect. In AD 1652, after Aurangzeb assumed charge as Governor of Deccan, he visited Agra and

Left and below, right and left: A farma of the pinnacle, which was fabricated to scale by Engineer E.W. Alexander during the monument's early restoration in 1874, is embedded in the floor outside the Jamaat Khana. The multiple narratives of the Taj Mahal are continuously evolving. On the floor of the Jamaat Khana, there is still evidence of a sketch plan of the dome; its slope and scale appeared to have been resolved on the floor looking up at the 'line of sight' of the dome towering above. Faint traces of writing in Persian or Urdu are yet to be translated but what is obvious are the sweeping lines which would have been drawn by the architect or contractor.

Facing page: The pinnacle of the Taj although replaced in the 19th century is as finely crafted as every other element in the building.

Vertical Section through the Taj

Left: A series of architectural drawings from the 18th century provide even today invaluable records of these monuments. The drawing in section of the dome and the crypt is critical to understanding the scale and detail in the Taj Mahal.

Facing page: This well-known very early painting of the Taj Mahal complex is an enormously important one as it shows Mehtab Bagh across the river in perfect alignment with the Taj Mahal, as an integral part of the grand design. Both gardens are well developed with thick plantation and functioning waterways. In Mehtab Bagh, the garden is fully established with a good cover of plants. The garden deviates here from the classical form of the Taj, with several more water channels. It also shows as many as three baradaris *on the waterfront and another two flanking the main northern gateway on the landward side. At the top left of the painting is visible the Agra Fort and perhaps at the top right is the Agah Khan Palace.*

inspected the Taj Mahal. In his letter written from Dholpur, just beyond Agra, he wrote about the badly needed repairs to the Taj Mahal: 'The building of this shrine enclosure of holy foundation is still firm and strong, except that the dome over the fragrant sepulchre leaks during the rainy season in two places on the north side. Likewise, the four arched portals, several of the recessed alcoves on the second storey and four small domes...have become dampened. The marble-covered terrace of the large dome of the holy tomb leaked in two places towards the north during the rainy season...the four northern compartments and seven arched underground chambers have developed cracks... It has been repaired, but it remains to be seen during the ensuing rainy season how far the operations prove successful. The domes of the mosque and the Jama'at Khana leaked during the rains... The master builders are of the opinion that if the roof of the second storey is reopened and dismantled and treated afresh with concrete, over which half a yard of mortar grout is laid, the semi-domed arches, the galleries and the smaller domes will probably become watertight but they are unable to suggest any measures of repairs to the main dome... Long-living protector! An evil eye has struck this model of lofty buildings. If the rays of your august attention fall on the remedy to ward it off, it will be proper.'[11] In less than 20 years, the dome of the holy tomb, the semi-domed arches, the four smaller domes and the domes of the mosque and the *Jamaat Khana*, all had developed defects. Clearly, there was a major effort, thereafter, to repair the domes but there are no records of that and today these problems seem resolved.

The tomb would be showcased in a perfect *char bagh*. On the 12th *Urz*, 1643, the main monument appeared complete. 'The *Paradise-like Garden* and a flower garden measuring 368 yards square abound in various kinds of fruit-bearing trees and rare aromatic herbs. Within the four walkways laid out in the middle of the garden which are 40 cubits in width, there runs a water channel, 6 yards wide, in which fountain up jets of water...from the Jamna. At the centre of this garden is a platform or *chabutra* 28 yards square around which runs the water channel. In the middle of the channels is a reservoir 16 yards square filled with water of the celestial Kauthar and provided with fountains all round it spouting jets of water illuminating as it were the world illuminating day...excellent features of this *jannat*-like garden such as its pathways fashioned entirely of red sandstone have reached a stage surpassing imagination.'[12] Lahauri's description

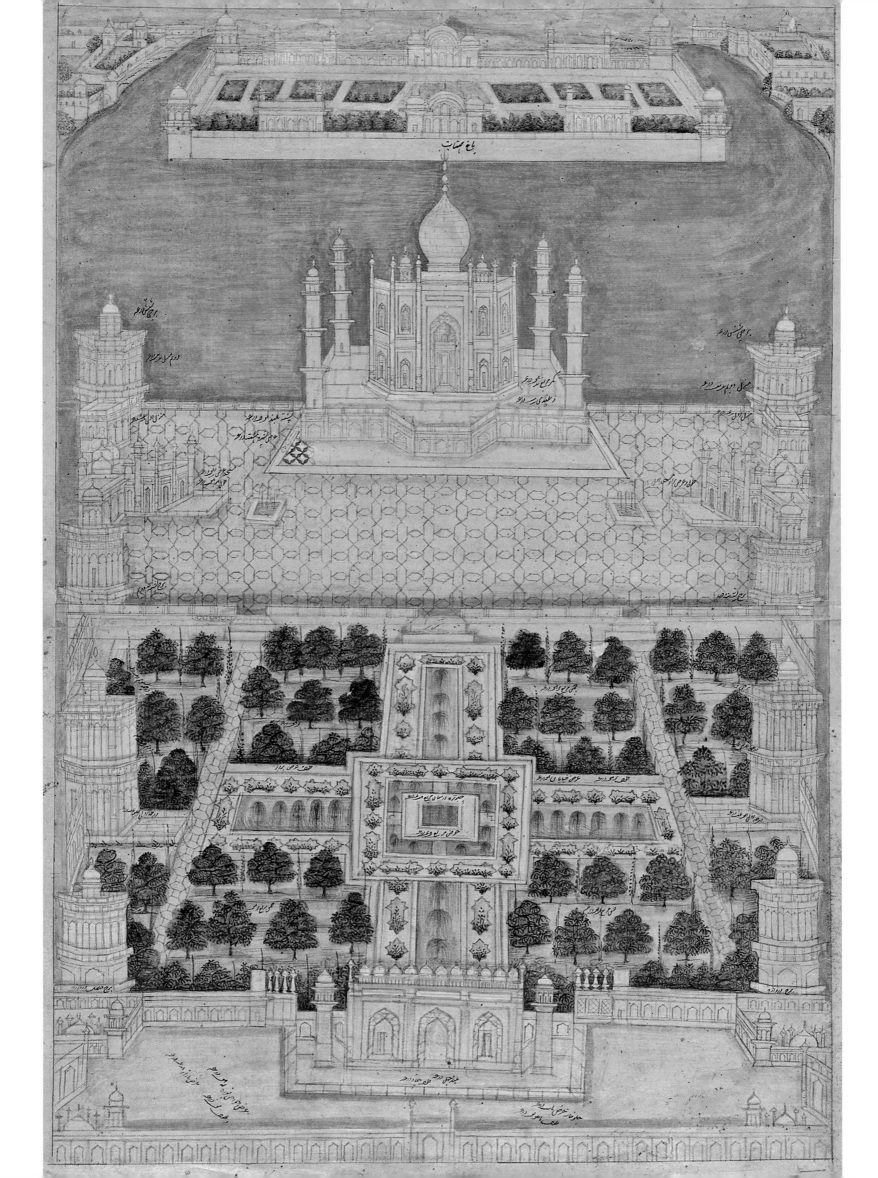

Above and facing page, top left: Mehtab Bagh was a lost garden and it was only in the 20th century that archaeological investigations revealed the remains of a burj *and wall in perfect alignment with the Taj Mahal. Soon, this gave rise to the story that Shah Jahan had planned to build a black Taj Mahal for himself across from the pristine white mausoleum of his wife. This story gained ground when noted British historian Percy Brown published a schematic grand design of what he perceived to be the emperor's original intent.*

of the gardens is far simpler than that of the tomb, perhaps, because the tomb was so splendid an achievement that all else seemed to pale into insignificance. There are almost no records of the plants which were so evocatively recorded in Babur's chronicles of Aram Bagh. There are, however, records of the produce of the garden being sold and mention of various kinds of fruit-bearing trees and rare aromatic herbs in relation to the garden. The garden is divided by water channels which intersect in a reflecting pond at the centre of the garden, and on either side is an *iwan* with three rooms now, perhaps, erroneously called the *Naubat Khana* which, in keeping with the symmetry, are mirror images of each other.

Across the river was Mehtab Bagh or Bagh-I-Mahtab Padshahi which has a classical *char bagh,* with its proportions similar to the scale in the Taj Mahal. This naturally fuelled the myth of the Black Taj – a twin across the river – a tomb the emperor intended for himself, perhaps perpetuated by folklore or by the evocative poetry that might have been inspired by viewing the Taj Mahal in the black reflecting pools at Mehtab Bagh on a moonlit night. However, the appearance of the illustration of the Black Taj in seminal treaties on the History of Architecture by Percy Brown only fuelled this idea among

historians and students of architecture alike. Fortunately, more recent excavations have revealed the true intentions of Mehtab Bagh – a critical component of the Taj Mahal Complex and one that weaves an even more powerful narrative than the idea of the Black Taj.

Mehtab Bagh's riverfront terrace has a large octagonal pool at its centre which, on a full-moon night, perfectly reflects the Taj Mahal. In this octagonal pool, measuring 88 feet across, with scalloped edges and 25 fountains, would the reflection of the Taj Mahal ripple in the moonlight? Would it be dark and brooding or shimmering white, the reflection ephemeral and even more symbolic of the emperor's intent? Below the reflecting pool is an *abshar-i-chadari* from which the water flowed into a second pool over a wall with tiers of tiny niches which would have been set with tiny lights. To the west was a water system comprising brick wells dug into the bed of the river near its edge from which a bamboo bucket and rope device lifted the water into cisterns, on a raised platform to collect the drawn water and then, to an aqueduct to transport the water to a large overhead tank adjacent to the southwest tower of the garden, from where it was disbursed.

Top, left middle and above: As late as the 1990s, the ASI in partnership with the Smithsonian Institute undertook detailed excavation and research of Mehtab Bagh to reveal the remains of the garden and the octagonal reflecting pond, its platform, a lower pond and a chaddar *connecting the two. Much of the original garden had been lost and Mehtab Bagh was buried under 300 years of silt deposits. The riverbed was now significantly higher than the garden.*

This is a system similar to the water system devised for the Taj Mahal gardens at Khan-e-Alam, though at a somewhat smaller scale. There were *baradaris* on the four sides at the end of the crossed water channels of which, only the foundations survive. Today, only the foundations of one of these *baradaris* which are in classical Shahjahani style, survive on the eastern side. Mehtab Bagh's glory was short lived as Aurangzeb recorded in 1652 'that the Bagh-I-Mahtab was completely inundated and, therefore, lost its charm...but the octagonal pool and pavilions around it are in splendid condition.'[13] However, even that was not to be; Mehtab Bagh was in the flood plain of the Yamuna across from the Taj Mahal, and over time, it was almost obliterated.

Mehtab Bagh was lost to floods for centuries. Only in the last 20 years has there been clarity that the emperor did not intend to build the legendary Black Taj for himself on the opposite bank but rather an even grander scheme which included the river as its central axis, with two *char baghs* on either side – a powerful and symbolically creative design gesture.

The design layout and production of what is arguably one of the world's grandest mausoleums, was for years claimed

Left: The tragic remains of the well foundation of the water-lifting system of Mehtab Bagh is testimony to a once grand garden plan.

Below: Mehtab Bagh, developed as part of the grand plan for the Taj Mahal, was short-lived as it was on the Yamuna flood plain and within a few years, was inundated, and still continues to be. It lies in perfect symmetrical alignment with the Taj and was intended perhaps to be used more as a pleasure garden from which to view the Taj, at that time a sacred space. It also had a water system similar to the Taj and the remains of the wells supporting the water system indicates how much the land and water levels have changed over the centuries.

Right: Directly across from the mausoleum lies the octagonal pond, a huge waterbody with some 26 fountains which when filled would have a reflection of the Taj, and when the fountains played, the reflection would be as ephemeral as it would be on the river. Water channels, chaddars and pathways made this an exceptional garden, a royal civic space as opposed to the sacredness across the river.

Right and below: The Taj Mahal complex was, at its peak, always bustling with activity. There were noblemen who paid obeisance, ladies of the zenana *who attended the prayers, imams who recited round the clock and* khadims, *the official caretakers of the site, who catered to everyone's individual needs. The gardens, therefore, were an integral part of the design, assuring cool pathways in the blazing heat of summer and redolent with fragrance and fruit in other seasons.*

These gardens were once covered with trees, bushes and fragrant flowers. Completely cleared in the early 20th century, they lost their meaning and sacred values as neither flowing water, fragrance nor fruit were retained.

by European travel writers to be a European conception. Geronimo Veroneo, a Venetian whose name gained great currency as the creator of this venture was recorded by Father Manrique as the architect of the Taj Mahal. He was, in fact, a jeweller who had presented himself in Shah Jahan's court and died while in Lahore. In the tradition of the time, his body was brought back to Agra and buried at the Christian cemetery with an unremarkable epitaph. It is unlikely that a Christian would have been employed to build this sacred space but so incredible was the Taj Mahal to those who visited it that it was believed it could only have been conceived by a European. Another legend was that Isa Muhammad Effendi was sent by the Sultan of Turkey to design the building, and some 200 years later, the design of the Taj is recorded in the *Tarikh-i-Taj Mahal* as his design. There is now clear evidence of Lahauri's work along with Ammanat Khan and others acknowledged in the Mughal Court records. However, from all scholarly accounts, the laurels for design and execution would go to the people who have rightly left their trace – the master craftsmen who lived and worked on the site, building the emperor's dream.

Besides the master craftsmen, hundreds of craftspeople were responsible for finally crafting the Taj Mahal. They brought to the process multiple skills and responsibilities, yet left little evidence of their contributions. The myths of their fingers being cut off and them being blinded so

Left: The funeral of Shah Jahan is an artist's impression as it is well known that on his death, Aurangzeb almost secreted his father's body away, transporting him by boat and interring him beside his wife in the lower crypt. There was no pomp and ceremony as would have befitted the Emperor of the World. On the facing page, the Taj is shown in part as a sacred space, with angels showering gold dust from above, while on the platform, European travellers or conquerors have appropriated the position of the Mughals, even lounging on the floor, with Indian servants on call, altering forever the intent of the mausoleum as a sacred space.

as to never imagine or engage with another building that could challenge the beauty of the Taj Mahal are perhaps folklore. The only evidence of their engagement then, perhaps, lies in the mason marks that are subtly present through the complex. But that subtle presence resonates even more powerfully today when we desperately seek narratives for the preservation of the Taj Mahal by engaging the community that are the true descendents of the people who crafted the Taj Mahal.

The mason-marks found in the Taj Mahal are engraved on red stone slabs, on the pathways, plinths and pavements but these are not seen on the white marble of the mausoleum. These have also been extensively used in other monuments of Agra, Fatehpur Sikri and Delhi. Similar evidence has been found in earlier Hindu architecture, so these were

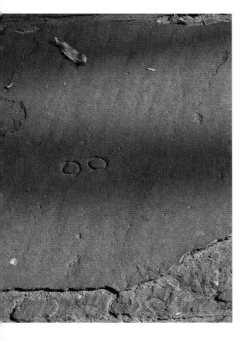

possibly a guild symboler, also believed to be an accounting system. In the Taj, the façades of the plinths often have entire names carved on them, perhaps denoting the master mason, while paving stones or step-risers have symbols which may have been the master mason's symbol for his workmen.

A variety of symbols were used. For instance, there have been many interpretations of the use of the *swastika*, although it should have been used in the reverse order. There are geometric symbols and even floral ones.

Architects, engineers and a variety of workers from several other disciplines would undoubtedly have left behind their individual symbols. The best-known one is Ammanat Khan's dating on the inscriptions over the mausoleum. There are perhaps many more yet to be fully analysed, making the Taj Mahal an unending enigma.

Carving in red sandstone reached its apogée under Shah Jahan although it was Akbar who after his victories in Gujarat brought craftsmen from there to build Fatehpur Sikri and much of Agra Fort. The resulting synthesis of styles and skills makes the heritage of Agra unique.

Following pages: This 1860 British line drawing shows a bucolic view of the Agra Fort waterfront with the river still used for navigation and leisure. Within a few decades the waterfront became industrialised altering this perspective and Agra city forever.

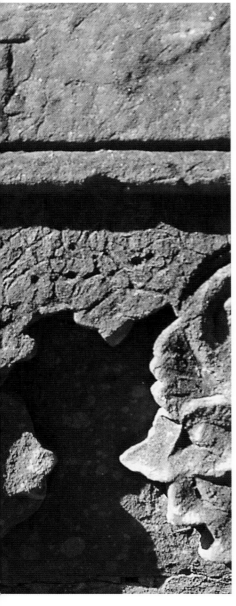

4

Changing Urban Landscapes

Today, in the dusty chaotic urban landscape of Agra, it is almost impossible to visualise elegant tree-covered pathways and grand mansions dominating the waterfront, or indeed the swiftly flowing Yamuna with fresh water from the melting snows of the Himalayas. Historically, Agra's fate has been linked to its ruler and as long as the seat of power was in Agra, it flourished, perhaps more for its rulers than the ruled but it's a fate which continues to dog its fortunes into the 21st century.

Four hundred years ago, Agra was considerably more cosmopolitan than it is now; the emperor's *omrah*s were not only Mughal but also Persian and Turkish. During Shah Jahan's reign, Agra was a sophisticated city to which travellers and merchants from around the world gravitated. Purveyors of exotic goods presented themselves at the court of the emperor. From Portuguese Jesuits to itinerant English traders, all were mesmerised by the scale and grandeur of the Mughal capital, previously unknown to them. When William Finch arrived in Agra in 1611, he was greeted by an English mercenary, three French soldiers, a Dutch engineer, and a Venetian merchant!

Agra was a hugely prosperous city at its peak during Akbar's reign. Artisans migrated from the villages to the city as patronage was assured. Silks, laces, gold and silver embroidery on turbans are mentioned in *Khulasat-ul-Tawarikh*. Akbar initiated the manufacture of carpets, even though merchants continued to import carpets, especially from Persia. In the imperial workshops, carpets over 20 yards in length and nearly seven yards wide were woven. Fabrics of great variety were woven in Agra and in the 16th and 17th centuries, it was the centre of indigo

Facing page: View of a pavilion at the Agra Fort – a favourite point to view the Taj Mahal by the British.

195

Right, above and below: The tomb of adventurer John William Hessing at Agra built in 1803 by his wife as a memorial to her husband is one of the more endearing legacies of the colonial era in Agra. Built in a miniature scale in the midst of the Roman Catholic Cemetery, it is an excellently crafted building complete with minarets and chhattris, of an era when Agra was still a melting pot of culture, and great craft skills.

manufacture. Agra and Fatehpur Sikri were important centres for pottery, ivory and metalworks, especially the production of swords, shields, daggers and chain armour of highly refined craftsmanship. By the time the Taj Mahal was built, stone craftsmanship had reached its zenith and became almost an industrial undertaking. Agra was the melting pot of skills from Hindustan and beyond as many converged here to create one of the world's finest buildings.

By the time Aurangzeb died in 1707, the Mughals had ruled Hindustan for a little over 180 years. Shah Jahan himself heralded the end of this great city when in the 1630s, he moved his capital to Delhi. He began constructing his magnificent new capital city even before the Taj Mahal was completed, shifting his handpicked overseer Makramat Khan and even Ammanat Khan, to administer the building of his new fort and city. The fate of Agra was truly sealed when the Peacock Throne moved to Delhi; the symbolism of this move was not lost on his nobles who also moved to Delhi to occupy the splendid mansions of Shahjahanabad. Shah Jahan had embarked on a spending spree and lifestyle of such excess that it eventually destroyed him and undoubtedly contributed in no small part to the ignominious end to his illustrious royal career.

Aurangzeb too left Agra and even Delhi untended as he battled the Deccan Sultanate and the Marathas; he remained away for most of his reign. The succession would be in disarray and although 11 Mughal emperors followed Aurangzeb, it was a lineage in decline as internecine battles led to a breakdown of the succession, and descendents gradually broke away. Aware of the weakened seat of power, Nadir Shah of Persia invaded Delhi in 1737 and capturing the Peacock Throne, effectively ended the Mughal rule. The Mughal Empire would be succeeded by a drastically different European Empire – one that would alter Hindustan but more so Agra irrevocably.

FOOTPRINTS ON THE CITY

During the 100 years which followed Aurangzeb's death, Agra was repeatedly plundered and what wasn't plundered and taken, began to simply fade away. Suraj Mal, the Jat ruler from Bharatpur was one of the more notorious looters and his booty prised out of the Taj Mahal and the Agra Fort was installed at his pleasure palace in Deeg. It was the Maratha power which survived in Agra but even though Scindia controlled the city, he did not live there. Instead, he appointed General Peron, his commander, a mercenary who

served in his army as Governor of Agra Fort and within a short time, he was replaced by Col. Hessing in 1799. Col. Hessing, once a Dutch commander, was now attached to Scindia. His term too was short-lived as he died in battle, defending the fort against the East India Company.

Although he had a brief tenure in Agra, clearly the impact of the Taj Mahal upon his family was significant and they built what they felt was a fitting memorial – a replica of the Taj Mahal in the Roman Catholic Cemetery at Agra. Constructed entirely of red sandstone, the tomb is a miniature compared to the Taj Mahal. Nonetheless, it stands some 3.4-metres high on a square platform. The tomb is a charming, if pretentious, adaptation and even contains a crypt with a corridor around it. Slender turrets are attached to the central *iwan* frame crowned by graceful pinnacles and a charming dome, topped with a *mahapadma* and *kalash*. Col. Hessing's epitaph somewhat pompously reads: 'When Colonel John William Hessing departed from this world, he left hundreds of scars of

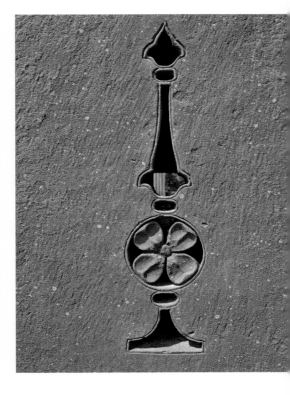

Above: The highly refined craftsmanship of Agra is evident in this finial detail on the façade of the tomb.

Below: The changes effected by the British in their use of the monuments was notable as in the early years there was little value for the great palace interiors. Largely used by troops, much of Agra Fort was defiled or built over. Assiduous conservation from the 20th century on has saved the buildings inside from being destroyed

separation. By person, he belonged to Holland and was born in that country. He gained fame in India, by the Grace of God.'

The year was 1803 and the East India Company was emerging as the force to contend with. Astute to the core, they installed Shah Alam, now blinded, as titular Mughal Emperor of India at Delhi. Agra began to transform from the once glorious capital of the Mughal Empire into a mofussil town, one of several which became the testing grounds where British traders honed their ruling aspirations. They occupied Agra Fort, captured its remaining treasures and within two years, laid out a cantonment around it.

In the years that followed, several urban transformation projects were undertaken. The Strand Road was constructed for famine relief in 1837 at the cost of the grand mansions along the edge of the river leading north from the Fort and ending in a huge park. It was a marked change from what impressed Bernier when he visited Agra some 200 years earlier: '...

Agra has more the appearance of a country town, especially when viewed from an eminence. The prospect it presents is rural, varied and agreeable, for the grandees having always made it a point to plant trees in their gardens and courts for the sake of shade, the mansions of *omrah*s, rajas, and others are all interspersed with luxuriant and green foliage, in the midst of which the lofty stone houses of Banyanes or Gentile merchants have the appearance of old castles buried in forests. Such a landscape yields peculiar pleasure in a hot and parched country, where the eye seeks verdure for refreshment and repose.'[1]

The Strand Road effectively erased the houses of the once powerful administrators and generals of the Mughal Empire. The house of Asaf Khan, Mumtaz Mahal's father and Shah Jahan's trusted chief minister was initially occupied by the East India Company officers but later, in 1857, was reputedly blown up along with other 'native' strongholds. The town hall and municipal offices reconstructed in 1881 occupy the site of Dara Shikoh's mansion. It was without doubt designed to ensure no *omrah* would ever wield power and influence or even return to the city. In the *History of Decorative Art in Mughal Architecture*, R. Nath made a scathing indictment of the East India Company when he said that of 270 beautiful monuments which existed at Agra alone, before its capture by Lake in 1803, barely 40 have survived. From being an exclusive Mughal capital, it now became a British secondary city, the cantonment, a new idiom for cities in India. These types of urban transformation were clearly instrumental in the colonisation process and often fundamentally altered not only power relationships within the urban landscape but more importantly, fine natural and social ecological balances that had often evolved over centuries.

During the First War of Indian Independence in 1857, Agra was ransacked and looted again and the British backlash was fierce as they sought to break the back of the 'native uprising'. Agra Fort became the garrison; barracks were built inside the once beautiful Fort and the marble pavilions became resident quarters for soldiers. The British officers fortified themselves inside Agra Fort for three months. Its commander died there and was buried in front of the Diwan-e-Aam. The implications were deep, but it was as much an overlay of history as was Akbar's reconstruction of the fort 200 years earlier. The 1857 War of Independence across India had profound implications as the East India Company was replaced and now India was part of the British Empire. Given the odds of controlling India

Above: Delicate marble screens, elaborately inlaid pillars and a secluded Sheesh Mahal, were notable in the fort. It was looted extensively after the collapse of the Mughal Empire; some pieces were transported to Deeg where these are now an integral part of its architecture. Another heavily inlaid pillar was removed to the house of the then Commissioner.

with a few hundred men and the dubious loyalty of rajas and their forces, the British redeveloped the cities to ensure the exclusion of unruly and threatening locals.

There were other transformations as well and it appears British occupants also needed to be compensated for the heat and dust of India, like Babur. His *char bagh* was now a guesthouse with a new floor, complete with awnings on the Jahangiri pavilions. East of the Taj, near the riverbank, the remains of a large palace and a walled garden were no longer visible. Lal Diwar, ruins of the palace of Khan Dauran Khan, the grand vizier, the *dargah* of Ahmad Bukhari and the remains of the tomb of Mumtaz Mahal's mother were all lost in the process of these acute transformations. Furthermore, Agra's citizens were divorced from the new rulers by a massive railway line which cut through the heart of the city and, as it became the centre of the north India railways, a swathe of railway land now separated the rulers and the ruled.

There were some important katras at Mumtazabad as Taj Ganj was then called: Katra Resham (top) was a market serai and a silk market frequented by the visitors who attended the observances at the Taj Mahal. Katra Omar Khan (above) was a large serai catering to the vast number of visitors to the Taj Mahal, and Katra Jogidas (top centre) was yet another prominent market serai.

Right, centre: A bungalow in Agra Cantonment after its thatched roof was removed revealed a tomb which had been appropriated as a residence. Much of Agra's heritage was similarly misappropriated.

Right: Monuments of the time varied vastly and even Akbar's favourite battle horse found a place in his commemorations, aptly situated on the road to Sikandra.

The creation of Strand Road too was the start of a new fate for the Yamuna. It had been the main waterway for transportation and there is enough evidence in old paintings to show it was a particularly busy waterway. But its once pure snow-fed waters were compromised as the use of the river and the relationship of the city to its riverfront altered irreversibly; the once sacred waters of the Yamuna were gradually contaminated with industrial effluent from the new industry that was now set up along the banks. So a great waterfront of pleasure gardens that had, over time, become a riverfront of funerary sites was once again altered, now facing a mass of industrial production sites along the river. With the introduction of the railways and the development

Top: Jahangir's pleasure pavilion had been 'renovated' and an additional floor added for the British troops.

Above: The same pavilion after the ASI removed the additional floor and restored the structure to its original.

of roads, there was a two-fold change – the river was no longer the main means of transport, and imported goods were easily transported into the city, undermining all the local production.

When Val. C. Princep visited Agra in 1867-68, he visited the jail which was the largest manufacturing unit for carpets: 'Here they have 2,400 human beings, all dressed alike. They all squat down as you pass, smack their hands and produce their prison number... The carpets here are very good – but not too good. As specimens of manufacture, they would hold their own against any carpets made...but I was obliged to confess, artistically they were a sad falling off from carpets of other places, which as manufacturers were much inferior... This place is one of the instances of well-intentioned effort failing from want of artistic knowledge.'[2]

In 1884, there were 65,000 artisans in the district and most of the Mughal craftsmen were still practising their traditional craft, especially shoes and metal ware. Taj Ganj too paled into insignificance from which it has not recovered but in the early 20th century, as India became the production centre of supplies for World War I, Agra's industries transformed as well to address the demands. Gradually, traditional industries went commercial, handmade shoes gave way to 'uppers' for boots for soldiers going to war, not unlike Akbar's demands but this marked the shift from hand-craft to semi-industrial production. Glass too was produced in huge quantities for export and fine carpets went into factory production. Great Mughal carpets gave way to everyday carpets. By World War II, industrial production along the waterfront had reached new heights as the city now served the interests of Empire at war.

Left and below: In the changing fortunes of Agra, as the fort was virtually abandoned, it wore a desolate look. Its grandeur diminished as the chajjas *and other decorative elements fell off. Yet it still dominated the landscape.*

By the late 19th century the surroundings of the fort were almost deserted, the moat had filled up and even the great entrance gateway had lost its dominance.

PARADISE LOST

Away from the city, the Taj Mahal too would be debased and yet preserved, the paradox rationalising the cultures at complete variance with each other. In 1972, David Carroll observed: 'The forts in Agra and Delhi were commandeered at the beginning of the nineteenth century and turned into military garrisons. Marble reliefs were torn down, gardens were trampled, and lines of ugly barracks, still standing today, were installed in their stead.'[3] Even the Taj Mahal was not spared as Carroll wrote: 'By the nineteenth century, its grounds were a favourite trysting place for young Englishmen and their ladies. Open-air balls were held on the marble terrace in front of the main door, and there, beneath Shah Jahan's lotus dome, brass bands um-pah-pahed and lords and ladies danced the quadrille.

The minarets became a popular site for suicide leaps, and the mosques on either side of the Taj were rented out as bungalows to honeymooners. The gardens of the Taj were especially popular for open-air frolics…'[4]

And the infamous story of Lord Bentinck, Governor of Bengal, undoubtedly consumed with greed for the potential worth of the Taj Mahal, decided it is said, to sell it off in amongst other bejewelled Mughal buildings and went so far as to announce plans to demolish and remove the marble façade and ship that to London, where it could be sold to members of the British aristocracy. While several of Shah Jahan's pavilions in the Red Fort at Delhi were stripped and the marble was shipped to England, plans to dismantle the Taj Mahal were abortive. The story, perhaps apocryphal, was

Below: The Taj Mahal and Agra Fort (bottom) were an artist's delight. In an era where drawing was a great skill, a vast number of paintings were produced. These are important as they show how the use of the monuments had changed. The Taj was clearly a pleasure park, its gardens and waterways offered respite to the colonial rulers from the heat of summer. While the fort retained its military function, the palaces served more mundane purposes.

that the first auction had not been a success, and all further sales were cancelled – it would not be worth the money to tear down the Taj Mahal. There is no proof of this story but it is one of the many narratives that have gained currency around the Taj Mahal. During this time, the brothers William and Thomas Daniell travelled through India and their paintings are perhaps amongst the best records of the monuments of India in the 18th century, especially of the Taj Mahal. These also form the basis for the picturesque, the philosophy of order which the new Empire brought to what was by now a rather dilapidated formality of the Mughal garden.

The British adopted the Mughal tradition of celebrating Empire in darbars and festivities, especially in Agra; the symbology was not lost on anyone. By the mid-19th century, the Taj had become a colonial 'pleasure resort'. Shah Jahan's perspective of representing *jannat* was lost. Looted, plundered and its sanctity compromised forever, the Taj Mahal stood mute witness to the dwindling fortunes of Agra of which it was the soul. Its immense wealth was gone without its protectors;

Above: As the East India Company was a virtually uncontrolled force that imposed its will on the country, the use and misuse of monuments previously held sacred was to change forever how we ourselves viewed the Taj Mahal as it became a destination for revelry and festivities.

Facing page: The arrival of the colonisers in Agra to replace local warlords and chieftains brought with it the pomp and ceremony which they perhaps adapted from India but which also made a travesty of the past.

Below: With the establishment of the ASI in the late 19th century began a period of recovery of Agra's cultural heritage. Monuments and sites were reclaimed by the state and rigorous conservation work began.

eunuch Agah Khan, its main custodian's home which once stood along its west side, was obliterated. There is almost no recorded history of what happened to the *khadims* who would have served the *rauza* even after the British took control of Agra. Desecrated by ignorance, soldiers of fortune and the arrogance of conquest, the description of the Maharaja of Gwalior's soirée at the Taj Mahal for his new masters, in Rousselet's account in 1875, speaks volumes on the changing landscape, marking the radical transition from sacred space to a completely desecrated site: 'On the night of the 15th, I took the road to the Taj asking myself whether it was not almost sacrilege to convert this tomb, which is one of the grandest monuments of India, into a place of amusement… We alighted from our carriage in the first court, before the monumental gateway leading to the garden, where the grenadiers of Scindia formed two lines between which we walked, passing under the immense pointed archway, from which hung a thousand lamps. From the high flight of steps, the garden appeared like a gigantic fairy scene; the fountains throwing up showers of glittering spray, the trees covered with fruits and flowers, the air filled with enchanting music from the orchestras. The long avenue paved with marble, presented a dazzling appearance. There were maharajas and rajas sparkling with diamonds; governors, diplomats, and officers covered with embroidery; Indian ministers and Rajput chiefs… Suddenly, at about 10 o'clock, there appeared at the farther end of the great avenue, a snow-white mass of colossal proportions, suspended in the air. It was the Taj which, till now hidden by the darkness had just been lit up with electric lights. The effect was magical. After this, the illumination became general and the *choubdars*, making their way among the groups of people, invited everyone to repair to the banqueting hall, the *Jawab* of the Taj, an immense apartment decorated with mosaics, where a Homeric repast was prepared, uniting the delicacies of Europe and Asia.'[5]

He describes the proceedings of the evening where Europeans ate and drank champagne while Indians stood apart as spectators. The cost of the evening to Scindia apparently was no less than Rs 20,000. Roussellet goes on to describe the finale: 'After the supper, there was a display of fireworks on the banks of the Jamuna. This river bathes the base of the Taj, describing a graceful curve round that monument; and numerous rockets of every description but all very ordinary, were reflected for an instant in the sheet of water. Scarely was all again enveloped in darkness when

a line of fire was seen floating down the Jamuna, lighting up the whole river. The effect was produced by innumerable little lamps thrown from the bridge of the Toundlah into the river, and thus covering it with a sheet of fire, which were carried along in the current... At midnight, we were entertained, with a brilliant concert from the English orchestras, and then the crowd gradually dispersed.'[6]

The sacred tomb was now in the domain of the profane; deep piety and recitations of the Quran had given way to dazzling orchestras.

Paradoxically, concurrent efforts were also made to restore the Taj Mahal. A young Captain Taylor had been appointed as early as 1810, just 100 years after Aurangzeb left Agra to its own devices, to repair the Taj Mahal. His responsibility was to restore the façades from where most of the jewels had been prised out and in four years he reported that he had completed this. By 1822, there was further damage to the façade and it was found that Taylor, far from restoring the jewelled inlay had replaced it with coloured *chunam*.

Following the 1857 uprising, there was a renewed effort to restore the Taj Mahal and over time, significant work was

Left, bottom left and right: The mausoleum had been looted and desecrated as invaders and marauders prised out its jewelled inlays. By the early 20th century, archaeologists and engineers began the painstaking work of restoring this prized monument to its original. This was no small task and then, as even now, the cost of scaffolding the monument almost exceeds the cost of conservation.

done, including replacing the inlay work on Shah Jahan's grave which had been vandalised during the uprising. Clearly, Taylor had also invested in the restoration of the garden as Princep notes on his visit (1867) to the Taj: 'The gardens are particularly well managed. There are two rose gardens and lawns quite English, with good turf.'[7] Princep further elaborates: 'Perhaps they may be out of place here but the green must be grateful even to the eye of the native, and to the Englishman recalls many pleasant places in the old country.'[8]

The fate of the Taj Mahal was, however, irreversibly altered when visited by the British Viceroy Lord Curzon at the turn of the century. He was genuinely overwhelmed by his first glimpse of the Taj Mahal 'designed like a palace and finished like a jewel – a snow-white emanation starting from a bed of cypresses and backed by a turquoise blue sky, pure perfect and unutterably lovely. One feels the same sensation as in gazing at a beautiful woman, who has that mixture of loveliness and sadness which is essential to the highest beauty.'[9]

Lord Curzon put an end to festivities because they were vandalising the Taj Mahal; he was profoundly aware of the misuse of the gardens where party-goers, revellers or vandals simply passed time, chipping away at the stones. 'It was not an uncommon thing, ' noted Curzon, 'for the revellers to arm

themselves with hammer and chisel, with which they whiled away the afternoon by chipping out fragments of agate and carnelian from the cenotaphs of the Emperor and his lamented Queen.'[10] The British often treated this as their private garden for their own nefarious purposes. The place was often strewn with drunken soldiers. In reality, much had already changed, the gardens were overgrown even though early in the 19th century, Fanny Parks wrote of the beauties of the gardens, the fine old trees with 'the odour of exotic flowers'[11] and the produce in fruit being very valuable. Curzon ordered a massive restoration project which was completed in 1908. His imprint on the Taj Mahal is a significant part of the layering of its history and, even though he was instrumental in reviving the ASI, he personally oversaw the restoration of the Taj. He also had to contend with the argument that a Christian administration had no role in preserving 'pagan monuments or the sanctuaries of older faiths.'[12] The future of monumental heritage in India was modulated by him: 'What is beautiful, what is historic, what tears the mask of the face of the past, and helps us to read its riddles, and to look it in the eyes – these, and not dogmas of a combative theology, are the principal criteria to which we must look.'[13]

There was much to be done to restore the monument. Clearly, the water channels had collapsed and there are detailed accounts of the immense repairs undertaken in this one-time massive restoration of India's most iconic site. In 1902, the original water system made with terracotta pipes was replaced with cast iron pipes which were connected to the main reservoir to restore a functional water system in the garden. By 1909, the water channels were embedded in concrete, followed by the thinning and replacement of old vegetation, consisting primarily of variegated palms, with more compact foliage. The thinning of trees was designed to provide vistas to the mausoleum, mosque and *Jamaat Khana*.

Significantly, it was the peripheral buildings, mosque and *Jamaat Khana* which needed the most restoration work. Sidhi Darwaza, Saheli Burj, the main gate and the colonnades around the *Jilau Khana,* were all painstakingly restored and even rebuilt. Silver doors which had been looted were replaced with teak doors. Curzon famously ordered a brass lamp inlaid in gold and silver from Cairo as he felt there was a cultural connection; this was installed over the cenotaphs as a present from him.

In this single restoration project, one can see the impact of divergent cultural contexts. Shah Jahan sought form and order within which the *rauza* would be situated in the attainment

Left and left, below: The transformative change during Lord Curzon's restoration efforts at the Taj was in the char bagh. *The gardens once filled with fruit and fragrance was overgrown by the early 20th century and Curzon ordered these to be cleared so it was easier to view the monument. The creation of an English lawn completely transformed the narrative and is now the accepted landscape of the Taj Mahal. The oval flower beds evoke the English country garden of the time. The lawn as a picturesque element was soon introduced in monuments across India, redefining how we viewed our own ideals of natural landscapes.*

Above, top and facing page: The Taj was always a much treasured icon of India's heritage. During World War II, an elaborate scaffolding was erected over the dome in an attempt to camouflage it during possible bomb attacks. British soldiers oversaw its construction with precision; the sacred mausoleum was now a mere monument.

of more sublime beliefs. By the time Curzon saw the Taj, the central path was, as described by Rousselet, an alley. To him, the overgrowth detracted from the pristine beauty of the Taj Mahal and he introduced the European ideal of the picturesque...the *rauza* of Mumtaz Mahal, the *jannat* of Shah Jahan's imagination became a monument with irreversibly altered values. In recent scholarly debates, discussions are afoot on whether to recreate the original garden but what will remain a mystery in this *char bagh* is the intent.

The British perspective of form and order was as influential as the Mughal one had been in its time. 'By 1905, a massive expenditure of 1,20,000 Pounds had been incurred in India; nearly half was spent in Agra and Fatehpur Sikri. Instead of a scruffy bazaar and dusty courts, a park now stood before the Taj. The mosques, tombs and arcades had been restored to the state in which they had been left by the masons of Shah Jahan. The discovery of old plans showing where the water channels once ran and the flowers bloomed, enabled the gardens to be laid out as they had once been.'[14]

According to David Carroll, ' To do this, a number of native artisans were trained to cut marble and to repair mosaics and were put to work, replacing the stones that had been plucked and hacked away by souvenir hunters. They patched the cracks in the minarets caused by an earthquake in the early part of the 19th century, and they polished the dingy marble walls. The stone channels were dug out, flower beds and avenues of trees were replanted, water from the Jumna River was once again circulated through the fountains.'[15]

Finally, in Curzon's words, the Taj was '...no longer approached through dust, wastes and squalid bazaars. A beautiful park takes their place; and the group of mosques and tombs, the arcaded streets and the grassy courts that precede the main buildings, are once more as nearly as possible what they were when completed by the masons of Shah Jahan. Every building in the garden enclosure of the Taj has been scrupulously repaired, and the discovery of old plans has enabled us to restore the water channels and flower beds in the garden more exactly to their original state.'[16] Curzon was pleased with his work: 'The central dome of the Taj is rising like some vast exhalation into the air,' he proclaimed in a speech given on the terrace of the Taj Mahal, 'and on the other side, the red rampart of the Fort stands like a crimson barricade against the sky... If I had never done anything else in India, I have written my name here, and the letters are a living joy.'[17]

Not only the Taj Mahal but many other monuments began to alter irreversibly. As they were protected, they began to be lost to the narrative of the city. Once, each building had a meaning and a perception in the eyes of the citizens; now they were simply great edifices.

Nonetheless, the ASI established ongoing programmes for restoration and recovery of the monuments of the Taj Mahal complex as well as Agra as many of the buildings were unable to withstand the ravages of time.

Following Curzon's interventions, the ASI was assigned extensive repairs and maintenance at the Taj Mahal; the paradigm for restoration was established, no longer by skilled master masons but by archaeologists and engineers. While the buildings were fairly restored, the imagination of the gardens was lost forever. The picturesque English garden superseded the exotic but possibly overblown Mughal garden and lawns, now part of the layering of the history of the monument, its secrets, its fragrances and the entire allegory transformed to a prosaic frame for the monument. J.H. Marshall in his defining *Conservation Manual* of 1923 which rigidly governs conservation in India, was of the view that 'to preserve the essential character of the original' in restoring Indian gardens, 'it is not necessary to attempt to reproduce with pedantic accuracy the original appearance of the garden in all its particulars.'[18] And so the die was cast from Vijaynagaram in south India to the *char baghs* of Agra. The English lawn now defined historic landscapes.

TAJ MAHAL AND AGRA IN THEIR CHANGING AVATARS

Today, the Taj Mahal is an oasis in a city overburdened and degraded and although the huge green space around the monument offers to the citizens respite from urban pressures, and while many of the residents of Agra still seek refuge in its serene environs, away from the noise and chaos, its fate still remains uncertain in its changing avatars. There are a slew of issues which the city needs to address to restore the relationship between the city and its heritage. The interdependence of the citizens and their heritage was largely economic; without that the city has floundered. The future of the city whose heart and very identity hinges on the Taj Mahal requires breadth of vision and great commitment.

Cities across India have faced immense challenges where development has been in conflict with the preservation of memory and the conservation of the past. With the Taj Mahal, secure behind its high walls and the ASI firmly mediating a very focussed path to restore and conserve this heritage, the danger of the monument being isolated from its context is very real.

Outside the Taj Mahal, beyond the sphere of its protectors lies a rudderless city without a renewed imagination about its future. Delhi remained the capital of independent India and Agra, a small and insignificant mid-sized town continued to survive its many avatars by adjusting to the reality of the contemporary landscape that emerged around it. Traditional industries gave way to small-scale workshops; metal workers once making swords established *ad hoc* foundries; brick kilns catered to the emerging middle class building their homes and tanneries served shoe factories that had replaced the cobblers making shoes for Akbar's army. Agra indeed reflects how cities in India have coped with the transition of royal patronage to a robust democracy. It is the quintessential small town of contemporary India, omnipresent as a resource of historical and cultural memory that would remain unsung, were it not for the Taj Mahal.

Agra was sadly impacted during the Partition of India in 1947 when its communities were fissured as its Muslim population fled to Pakistan. Life was once again irrevocably altered in 1984 when the pressures of development resulted in a Petroleum Refinery being built some 60 kms north of Agra in Mathura. A Public Interest Litigation (PIL) was filed as it was felt that sulphur dioxide emissions would permanently damage and discolour the Taj Mahal. The concern regarding

217

Below and bottom: The landscape of Agra was also to irrevocably change. Once known as the 'emporium of the traffic of the world' after India's capital shifted to Delhi, Agra became a backwater. The city once rich in art and craft, poetry and music, military warfare and trade, Agra became a small-town industrial hub and its eminence in India's landscape was never restored.

the environmental threat to the Taj has been articulated in the landmark judgement of Hon'ble Justice Shri Kuldeep Singh dated 30/12/96: 'The Taj is threatened with deterioration and damage not only by the traditional causes of decay but also by the changing social and economic conditions which aggravate the situation with even more formidable phenomena of damage and destruction.'[19]

In a seminal judgement in 1994, the Supreme Court ordered fierce pollution emission controls on the refinery. Previously unknown zero emissions were mandated and to be monitored in perpetuity. It went a step further to examine the crisis of urban pollution which would impact the monument and some 450 small-scale industries were ordered out of Agra. Highways were to be diverted, tanneries and brick kilns were closed and, effectively, the emporium of the traffic of the world was on notice. Traditional skills which had adapted to the changing economic order had to move 50 kms away from the Taj Mahal. Of course, remedial measures such as electricity, sewage and sanitation were to be provided across the board to reduce the impact of urban pollutants but for the residents who lived here for generations, there was little remission. The mandate was unusual – no industry would be permissible within a 50-km radius in what is now known as the Taj Trapezium and a 500-metre radius green zone around the Taj Mahal. Huge tracts of land were to be forested as added protection.

The fate of Agra was sealed: the Taj Mahal was protected but the back of its economy was broken. Over one-and-a-half million people were affected directly and, perhaps some three million indirectly. As industries shut down, factories were sealed and kilns and tanneries breathed their last. Agra was in complete decline. Over time, the city has, as always, recovered. Under the scrutiny of a monitoring committee of the court, the highway no longer traverses the city centre and a massive waste-water drain runs along the edge of the Yamuna some 15 feet above the riverbed to address the problem of effluents contaminating the river. Strand Road now is a major connector linking the Taj Mahal to the Yamuna Expressway, a highway designed to bring tourists to the Taj Mahal, elevated above its decayed landscape of abandoned factories, and battered buildings which have survived the ravages of time – an eloquent reminder of Agra's more elegant past.

In a curious irony of our times, initiatives to protect the Taj Mahal would finally provide a healthier environment for its citizens. Even more recently, concerns of security have

consumed the world and this too has impacted the Taj Mahal. It was proposed that it would be ideal to clear the precinct of the Taj Mahal of any habitation so that security could be better managed and once again the spectre of dislocation and loss loomed over the citizens. It was even suggested that the entire Taj Ganj be cleared of habitation. Fortunately, better sense prevailed and Taj Ganj survived, a vestige of the past grappling with the present.

The Taj Mahal's beauty and fame remain undiminished – it was India's first World Heritage Site and remains India's best protected monument. However, as visitors to the Taj Mahal grew over time, more of its secret spaces were closed to public; no longer could they climb the minarets; in the mausoleum itself, the upper levels were closed to public while the graves and the marble screen are barriered with aluminium mesh screens, vitiating what was once a sacred journey. The multiple narratives of the Taj Mahal today often attain comic proportions in the stories of tour guides who love the Taj but diminish its presence.

Above: Agra has faced multiple misfortunes since it ceased to be the centre of the Mughal Empire. Even as patronage and trade changed the city fortunes, invasions and loot destroyed it further. Devastating floods in 1922 inundated the monuments along the riverside. Undoubtedly, the city too would have been flooded – a precarious livelihood at continuous risk.

Following pages: The mass of planting around the Taj Mahal is exceptional by any standard and provides an ecologically sound buffer to protect the environment of the Taj Mahal.

The historic Supreme Court judgement of 1994 ordering a 500-metre green buffer zone, has without doubt been the single most valuable tool for the preservation of the Taj Mahal. While it may not have served Agra's citizens so well, it has provided an unarguable protection mechanism for the future of the Taj Mahal.

Epilogue
The Future of the Taj Mahal

As the world's most famous tomb, the Taj Mahal has fascinated humanity over time. However, this monument is not a dominating feature of a great urban skyline like the Statue of Liberty, the Eiffel Tower, or St. Paul's Cathedral, but is usually approached unseen, and is dramatically revealed and experienced on entering the site. It is the enacting of the experience of walking through the portals into the garden and approaching the Taj Mahal that makes it special – an experiential moment perceived from within rather than from distant vistas. This intrinsic isolation, by design, from the city, as an exclusive compound to be discovered, has always disconnected it from the daily lives and lived imagination of the citizens of Agra.

Despite this non-exertive presence on the Agra skyline, the Taj Mahal has remained the symbol of the entire nation. Appropriated and consumed by one and all, it is perhaps India's most used symbol of beauty, elegance and excellence. Transcending barriers, it cuts across communities and singular visions to represent the rich cultural diversity of India. Its significance as the most important image of India remains undisputed. And as one of the most famous buildings in the world and the most renowned and recognised icon of India, there have been innumerable symbolic and metaphoric ways in which the Taj has been exploited. Perhaps no building has lost itself to advertising as much as the Taj Mahal. Donald Trump has appropriated the name for his casino in Las Vegas; a blues singer and countless Indian restaurants throughout the world have used its name too. Its image is found on frozen food packets, displayed at barber and tailor shops, and embossed on ornaments of every kind. As a signifier of quality and magnificence, the site continues to be used in a host of metaphorical ways. It sells tea; it became the marketing symbol of India's earliest hotel chain and features

Below: It is the impulsion to protect the Taj from the changing political, social and economic conditions that subject it to threats, and the wear and tear of declining economies that has now pervaded its context. Apart from the Taj, monuments tucked into every neighbourhood, settlements still in their original form, are all vulnerable in the new world order, uncertain in the present as much as the future.

in Bollywood spectacles. Such representational practices have rendered the building something of a cliché, signifying quintessential luxury, quality, romance and splendour. However, for some historians, it's also a symbol of exploitation, of labour under cruel and inhuman conditions that produced the masterpiece in marble. It has perpetually been caught in this double bind that haunts its very preservation, making it a very challenging and complex monument and, more importantly, historic site to deal with.

In fact, its preservation narrative today is as much about its protection from within as from the outside. From within, the quest has always been to extend its material fabric and protect the very texture of the marble, its ornament, inlay work, adjoining buildings and its gardens as a comprehensive experience. From the outside, it is the impulsion to protect it from the changing political, social and economic conditions that subject it to threats ranging from terrorism to pollution, and the wear and tear of declining economies that has now pervaded its context. It is this imagination and reading of the changing context within which the Taj Mahal is situated, which will be critical to safeguarding its existence in the future. Put simply, the future of the Taj Mahal depends on the future of Agra.

The city functions as much for its large rural population that exists at its edges. Across India, development is transforming cities at an alarming pace but has not yet transformed Agra for multiple reasons.

Below: The river too has receded. No longer the fresh-flowing Himalayan waters, today the river is a turbid stream, flowing at a distance from the mausoleum and virtually unnavigable. Additionally the emperor's entrance to the Taj Mahal is lost forever; its very base now lies many feet below the present ground level. Yet it still presides over the landscape.

Today, measures to protect the Taj Mahal are continuously upgraded as gunmen parade its bastions and the Central Industrial Security Force responsible for the security of this monument (CISF) raises its flag at the entrance gateway. Housed in the cloisters at the entrance to the Taj Mahal, the presence of the CISF now makes the forecourts resemble a cantonment with extensive military presence and the related paraphernalia for security, and not the sacred threshold to India's most exquisite mausoleum. The issues are aplenty – the public can view the Taj by moonlight from the main gate half a kilometre away; the forecourt paved over with concrete, some three or four decades earlier, to provide access for visiting dignitaries was levelled over the steps to the main entrance while the red sandstone water channels in the gardens were painted blue to create the impression of water. The gardens since Lord Curzon's interventions completely obliterate any

resemblance to the idea of the gardens of *jannat*; court orders to create a green buffer zone resulted in trees planted against the Taj's outer walls, their roots threatening its very foundations; a display called 'The March of Indian Civilisation' installed in the cloisters of the main complex draws visitors into a pan-India imaginary, distracting them from the rich narratives about the Taj Mahal that could add to their immediate experience of being there. Most critically, the custodians of this monument rarely if ever dialogue with the citizens of Agra on how best this site can be preserved, what their stake is and how they could partner in the protection and presentation of this site. The Taj Mahal is all that it has come to symbolise but so much more of its many facets are so rarely explored. And the overwhelming number of visitors poses new threats, not of pollution but of simply wearing the monument down – the challenges ahead are daunting.

Following pages: Thousands of little Taj Mahals are a tourist's delight. Not always made of marble but often soapstone, yet every detail is finely crafted. They are the contemporary souvenier for the millions of Indians who throng the Taj annually.

THE TRANSFORMATION OF AGRA

The most profound change that is the biggest threat to the monument is the city of Agra itself and its future, for that is intrinsically linked to the future of the Taj Mahal. It is important to address the urban issues that have a direct and often irreversible impact on the monument. The city of Agra is home to over 1.7 million people and host to over 6 million visitors annually. It continues to suffer from a chronic shortage of power which has resulted in the informal sector economies becoming dependent on individual diesel generators, once again shooting up pollution levels in the city. Despite court orders to ensure the most rudimentary infrastructure to the city, it still faces acute shortage of basic amenities. Its residents receive a few hours of water supply daily while the River Yamuna is today no more than a turbid rivulet, rendered so because cities like Delhi and other towns upstream continue to disgorge huge quantities of untreated waste into the river. For much of the year, the river is stagnant, with most of its water having been drawn to meet the needs of India's capital city. The Supreme Court's orders have been implemented in Agra and all the waste is now removed but has failed to address the upstream problems of the river which impacts the city – indeed a far cry from the snow-fed waters which attracted the Mughal settlement and Shah Jahan to imagine a *jannat* on earth.

Today, the ideas of a buffer zone intended to protect the Taj can at best be seen as a short-term holding strategy to safeguard the integrity of the surrounding of the Taj Mahal. However, in essence, they are mechanisms, in the long view, of separating rather connecting – especially the community that forms the broader ecology in which the Taj Mahal and several other important monuments in Agra are located. Essentially, the major challenge faced by the contemporary custodians of India's heritage is how to embrace rather than isolate surrounding communities – the true inheritors of this heritage. Unfortunately, the contemporary Institutes for heritage protections in India are strangled by an archaic system of decision-making, and huge shortage of manpower. Partnerships and outsourcing of studies only further accentuate the lacuna, both physical and intellectual. The current government policy of not recruiting or even investing in its manpower, has in terms of the appropriate skills, exposed a conundrum. In this context, the ASI is the nodal agency to discharge Government's constitutional

responsibility to safeguard the nation's heritage. Partnerships with Government are not for ordinary entrepreneurs; they require the tenacity of organisations and their unflinching commitment to preserving India's heritage. Unlike green field industrial projects, a heritage site carries with it histories and cultural associations that require sensitivity, strategy and consensus-building that are complex and unpredictable as a process. Thus the commitment to this process requires determination of engagement, completely different in approach and protocols involved in a green field enterprise. Safeguarding it today requires tremendous effort of public and private agencies, not as a narrow service to Government or any private enterprise but indeed to every Indian.

REIMAGINING THE TAJ MAHAL AND ITS CONTEXT

'The future of the monumental heritage of Agra will only be secure within a civic order which first provides for the well-being of the citizens and imbues them with a sense of pride.' The vision statement of the Blue Ribbon Panel of the Indo-US Joint Mission in 1995 remains as valid today as it was 21 years ago. It is equally important to recognise that the vision of the panel inextricably links the fate of the monument to that of the city, a vision born out of profound concern for the citizens of Agra, whose futures are as fragile and unsustainable in its present condition. While the presence in their midst of a World Heritage Site is an obvious advantage, it is not leveraged in any way to enrich their cultural, social and economic ecology.

Tourism in Agra has grown exponentially, not just in terms of international but also domestic tourists. Economic development and communication have made travel within India relatively easy for all Indians. Thus, the volume of domestic travellers to Agra, and indeed the Taj Mahal has already exceeded what the monuments can sustain. Today, 6 million tourists visit the Taj Mahal every year; approximately 30% of the tourists are foreign and 70% are Indian. Of the ASI's income of Rs 25.3 crores for Agra, approximately half comes from the income of entrance tickets to the Taj Mahal. The Agra Development Authority (ADA) earns Rs 25 crores from the Taj Mahal and nothing goes back for its upkeep – only the ASI spends Rs 3 crores independently a year to look after the the Taj Mahal. Thus, even the economic model of subsidies that surround the Taj Mahal does not privilege the monument, leave alone its position within the larger ecology of Agra. This lopsided emphasis on the deployment of funds for the monument and the uneven relationship between the city authority and the custodians of the monument, is emblematic of the larger disjuncture in the conflicting relationships that exist between institutional authorities for their concern for the Taj Mahal.

However, this conflict plays itself out, interestingly, in more contradictory terms in the broader context of the Taj Mahal – from the adjacent Taj Ganj area to other settlements in the vicinity. According to a report by the Centre for Urban and Regional Excellence (CURE), Agra has 432 slum communities with a population of over 8,50,000[1] people. Of these, 168 settlements lie in the vicinity of historic sites and nearly 40 per cent of these settlements do not have access to water or sanitation. Thus, most households extract ground water,

Facing page: The city teems with historic buildings; each played and, in some cases, continues to play a role in the life of the city. Archways still define precincts as clearly as they did then as activities often continue in the same space, more by custom and tradition.

Preceding pages: The riverfront of Agra seems frozen in time, with the foundries and factories closed under the court orders. Highways and expressways cut into the city's fabric, catapulting tourists into the Taj and evading the city.

Above: In Kachhpura, which still is a largely rural settlement wedged between the Humayun Mosque and Mehtab Bagh, a historic structure has found a new use as a school, with the eponymous name, 'Basic Vidhyalay Kachhpura'.

Top: Buildings from a more elegant time remain as fragments of remembrance; once structures like this had an important role in the life of the city.

both depleting the natural water table and natural aquifers, and often polluting them. Interestingly, in the proximity of these settlements often lie some significant historic sites, less known because there is no access. While this sprinkling of sites is embedded in the lived lives of the community, they gain no public attention and, thus, are not leveraged in any way to benefit the community.

Zooming out to view the city makes these contradictions even more acute. While the Taj Mahal today is a realisable destination for every Indian, indeed every world traveller, the city which houses this majestic monument is overburdened and degraded, unable to support its own population, much less its visitors. The Jamuna reflects the crisis as it is at its most stagnant in Agra. Devoid of adequate water for most of the year, the riverbed is in any case extremely contaminated, and has become a site for informal production activities. More than a river, it can be seen as a site for *ad hoc* manufacture and services for the informal and unregulated economy. These activities range from laundry to textile dying, small-scale auto repair and industrial fabrication – each polluting to different degrees and further degrading the embattled river – a sort of no-man's land or interstitial space that lends itself easily to informal appropriation.

Traffic jams are a common sight, thus discouraging tourists and even residents from traversing the city, further isolating the few sites on tourist itineraries from the rest of the city. Public transportation is virtually non-existent and the bus service is woefully inadequate, thus encouraging auto rickshaws and other vehicles – all contributing to air pollution. The response of the State has been uneven, while there is alternative fuel provision for some industries, the informal sector remains vulnerable with an uncertain future. So while steps to create the trapezoidal delineation of a zone protected from industry, and the shutting down of industries within this zone, were seen as measures that would save the Taj Mahal, in reality, the life of the city and its economic challenges are striking back, albeit in small measure that may be harder to control. The decline of the economy of the city, in effect, only further exacerbates pollution that we heap on our cities and, by extension, on our heritage.

We, therefore, need to look at our cultural heritage in its broadest and most inclusive terms. Culture is not static or even quantifiable; it is both traditional and contemporary but, most importantly, an implicit set of rules that evolves within

Above and facing page, middle and below: Agra is a vigorously urban yet charmingly rural city, and both are situated seamlessly within each other. Measures to protect the Taj Mahal have impacted the development of the city as implicitly as they did 400 years ago when the capital shifted to Delhi. Life in the city moves at a relatively gentle pace, with no industry permitted within a 50-kilometre radius. Employment opportunities are few as alternative growth opportunities have bypassed their development paradigm.

Facing page, above: The riverfront gardens of Agra are a mere fragment of the past. Only four gardens protected by the ASI are still intact. The others have become successful nurseries, supplying plants all over India. The historic buildings, pavilions, water channels, burjs and wells inside them are in an advanced state of decay and would require herculean efforts to restore.

a society at a given moment in time. Appreciation and respect of this is the basis for any discussion on the future of the Taj Mahal. It is critical to be able to understand the complexities of societies in transition, the conflicting objectives of traditional cultures and aspirations of modernity. Our ability to address the imperatives of change while securing the cultural heritage resources and building upon it, will be the basis for any successful intervention. The management of change is effectively the opportunity for a dynamic process of linking the threads of the past with a vision for the future. And it is only through this more complex engagement with the condition that we will be able to evolve a sound strategy to safeguard the future of the Taj Mahal.

What then constitutes a cultural reading of the contemporary condition of cities like Agra or, for that matter, any contemporary city in India? In this dynamic context, if the production or preservation of architecture or urban form has to be informed by a specific reading of cultural significance, it will necessarily have to, in the broader planning debates, be relevant. In fact, an understanding that 'cultural reading' evolves, will challenge as well as clarify the role of conservation agencies and activists as advocates willing to also engage with questions of growth and change (versus a preservationist who opposes change) – that is, institutional structures need to engage with both the historic and contemporary on equal terms. Under such conditions, a draining of the symbolic import of the historic landscape will potentially lead to a deepening

of ties between heritage and contemporary realities and experiences. This approach will allow historic buildings and urban typologies to be transformed through intervention, and placed in the service of contemporary life, realities, and emerging aspirations. Here, the historic landscape of the city will embrace the contemporary city and be informed, remade and, most importantly, preserved by its logic. In the case of Agra, this question is critical in not only creating a common platform for varied agencies such as the ADA and ASI to operate and collaborate, but also for the contemporary urban issues in Agra to be accorded the same attention as the privilege that its protected heritage landscapes have had for decades. It is in this condition then the questions of sanitation and water could be linked to questions of material conservation and visitor management – not privileging one over the other but rather recognising their interconnectedness!

In the context of contemporary Agra and the many conflicting visions that surround it, how does one prioritise? Visions that come to mind are as diverse as the now infamous Taj Heritage Corridor which proposed to reclaim the riverbed to create shopping malls, where the 'Brand' of the Taj Mahal is appropriated for commercial and real estate gains by the State! That is an imagination where even the Taj Mahal is perceived as a mere brand to leverage strategically for short-term profit even if that means compromising the integrity of the site – a strategy totally incompatible not only with the intrinsic qualities of the site but with the commitment of the nation-state to safeguard the monument as a World Heritage Site.

On the other hand are the visions, experiences and preoccupations of the domestic tourists. For them, this is a pilgrimage, often via Mathura or Ajmer Sharif, and they often offer money at the tomb, or touch the tomb and then their hearts or foreheads – a gesture of reverence that cuts across all religions. They don't perceive this as a heritage site or city, rather a point of interest and perhaps deep reverence. Of the 1.8 million domestic tourists, 90 per cent fall in this category. One should equally acknowledge the use of the mosque of the Taj Mahal, to this day, for Friday prayers by the local community. Even today, the Taj Mahal is closed to visitors on Friday while the mosque remains central to the life of the citizens of Agra. For the remaining domestic travellers and the 300,000-odd foreign tourists, the significance is historic and the experience aesthetic, an experience which either serves as a pilgrimage to celebrate their own love story, of love manifest

in the millions of portraits of couples, lovers and friends with the monument as a backdrop, or the millions of 'selfies' today, constructed by the self-possessed younger generation obsessed about celebrating their presences at the Taj Mahal through social media.

So how do we construct a contemporary and relevant narrative to define Agra's heritage in this varied condition? If we treat 'significance' as static and follow the regular strategies, we will not only diminish further the potential resonance of the monument globally but also in its own immediate context of the city of Agra. If, however, we open the context to insensitive new constructions of significance, it would mean opening a Pandora's box. Thus, in the process of interrogating the construction of new significances, the role of institutions and individuals becomes even more critical, where one has to negotiate a fine balance between draining these sites of their ideological symbolism and meaning while keeping the illusion of the architecture and the urban fabric intact. It is not then a matter of using only the past and the historic narratives to inform conservation strategies but of finding new ways of using newer contemporary narratives and aspiration to inform the agendas for conservation in the present. These would range from new facilities and centres for interpretation amongst other things but also evolve strategies that help address issues of contemporary economies and the well-being of the people who create and support the ecology within which the site is located, rather than isolate these issues almost premised on the non-recognition of the current reality.

The buffer zones to protect the Taj Mahal are a classic case in point where the stricter the buffer zones, the more isolated the city is from the monument, as then, the monument belongs to some abstract entity or authority. Essentially, what these designations do is cause parts of the city to secede from the urban context for the cause of national or international interest. Naturally, in the perception of the city, this is not a cause in their interest or well-being. As the city decays, the value of the Taj Mahal for the local citizen will decrease, further exacerbating the already tenuous relationship the monument has with its context. So while, through these isolationist policies that are often object-centric, the level and ability to engage with good as well as competent material conservation (which is important) will improve the broader health of the monument, the ecology the monument is set in will diminish.

Left, below and bottom: The Taj Mahal is and always will remain the focus of Agra and its fortunes. Tourism promotion has yet to engage with its citizens or indeed add value to their economies. The transformative change in the years ahead will be in merging the two realities.

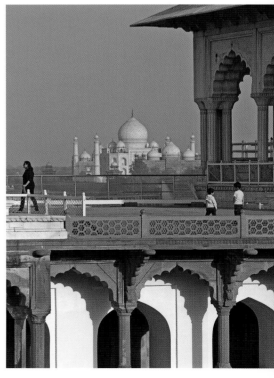

237

Preceding pages: It is not a matter of using only the past and the historic narratives to inform conservation strategies but of finding new ways of using newer contemporary narratives and aspiration to inform the agendas for conservation in the present. If one were to simply look at the panorama of Agra, there is yet so much opportunity for sustainable development. The Taj Mahal will remain the centre of Agra, it needs to become the centre of its people.

This strategy cannot conserve the context the building is set in. Thus, the broader economy, robustness of the cultural landscape and the functioning of the broader urban system of Agra become a crucial issue, for, the health of the stakeholders is as important as that of the monument.

It is here that the ASI and the ADA and other such concerned authorities have to leverage partnerships with private enterprises to engage with the city and its stakeholders in a more substantial way. Status quo, while easy to maintain is no longer going to be sufficient to manage the multiple pressures faced by the monument and the city. All the intellectual and scientific resources of the custodians require to be mobilised to enable a robust dialogue and broader engagement. How, within current institutional frameworks, might this work? And more importantly, how can the framing of the problem be widened in ways that these questions can be addressed through newly designed public-private partnerships – one way of working beyond the current institutional frameworks? How can the institutional agendas be constructed at the intersection between conservation and urban development in Agra and urban India?

One possible way would be to expand or redefine the areas of protection and intervention not as an abstract geometric definition of the trapezoid or buffer zone but instead, by using the historic and cultural imagination to create zones of synergy rather than isolation. For a start, just including more mindfully the adjacent Taj Ganj area would be an expansion to what constitutes the World Heritage Site. The inclusion of Taj Ganj would do two fundamentally important things. Firstly, it would create a wonderful counterpoint to the singular monumentality of the Taj Mahal and bring into view and prominence lesser-known fragments of heritage that will only powerfully prop up the narratives that surround the Taj Mahal – the private built heritage of *serais*, the *darwazas* that define areas, the *mandis*, *tolas*, *padas*, *katras* that have been forgotten as they get embedded in the contemporary mutations that now characterise the image of Taj Ganj. This could be extended to make visible the geography of wells and water bodies that once made Agra such a robust urban system. Secondly, a re-articulation of the site would bring the community to the fore in terms of the lived experience of the site. It would also propel policies that include the community. The community at Taj Ganj includes 4,500 households, most of which can actually trace their existence to the making of the Taj Mahal. What a powerful tool this could potentially be for communicating the stories on the Taj through these oral histories and lived experience. This would be crucial as a project to enrich the experience and the long-term sustainability of the site – a strategy that would, in a single swoop, make the community central to this process of conserving the Taj Mahal, and establish that crucial link to the greater community.

Building on this expansion, the next critical step could be to scale up one more level, using the concentration of other historic sites as a parameter. The Yamuna riverfront once had 44 Mughal gardens and a vast number of mansions, lost today, strung along 6 kilometres of Yamuna's economic, cultural and hydrologic field. Could the river become central to this imagination once again not only as the arena for re-establishing the historically correct perceptions of the Taj Mahal but as a focus for re-establishing the monument centrally in the perception of the city? From a shift of framing such as this, perhaps what might emerge is the potential for more sustainable models of conservation not only of the Taj Mahal but of several other monuments lining the Yamuna by telescoping outwards from Agra's monuments into the larger

Facing page and below: The city has grown intensively around the Taj Mahal and once served a purpose. New narratives must link the future and the past. This should range from addressing the economic challenges of its citizens as well as affirmative action to restore confidence amongst its people. These would range from new facilities and centres for interpretation amongst other things but also evolve strategies that help address issues of contemporary economies and the well-being of the people who create and support the ecology within which the site is located.

Following pages: The transformation of the River Yamuna from an idyllic waterway (below) to the way it is today (bottom) demands a much more expansive response to the city's future.

241

Below: There needs to be a collective effort to revitalise the economy of Agra. Industries languish 30 years after closure. A robust approach to their reuse, even as commercial establishments could fuel the city's economy. Such a vision would provide an alternative to the semi urban chaos (bottom) which seems to have overtaken most of the city.

landscape and region. By partnering with multiple scales of Government, non-governmental, academic communities and civil society more generally, the possibilities for productive economic and administrative synergies could also emerge.

Such speculations – the true mandate of urban planning – would draw conservation closer to the process of city governance and result in strategies and interventions for cultural, ecological and economic conservation by negotiating between three scales: Agra and the Yamuna as larger territorial zones of social, cultural, ecologic and economic importance; the Yamuna as a spine for Mughal monuments, gardens and appropriations, including nurseries and contemporary settlements, and at the architectural scale of individual sites along the river such as Ram Bagh, Chini ka Rauza, Itimad-ud-Daulah's tomb, etc. As a non-contested zone, the Yamuna presents the easiest point of entry to consolidate and reimagine the social and cultural activities in Agra's landscape of Mughal era monuments and garden sites as well as their transformations over the past 400 years.

The river itself is a site for rejuvenation for imagination and conservation of Agra. From a landscape of pleasure and crafts to manufacturing, heavy industry and transportation corridors, Agra's Yamuna bears marks of its transformation in serving the Mughal, British and Indian regimes. How might this landscape again be transformed to multiply cultural and ecological conservation goals and intensify economic activity within the Agra region? What programmes and types of landscapes should be developed within the Yamuna basin – water transportation for access to monuments, physical access for recreation, circulation, agriculture, productive landscapes to cleanse and treat the water? How might a collection of various garden and monument sites be integrated into a comprehensive 'network' which can also increase the resilience of physical monuments and intangible heritage within Agra? How might fragments from other phases in Agra's land use history, such as industrial facilities along the river built in the British colonial era be integrated into this 'network'? What are the potential programmes for primary and secondary sites within this network – community centres, educational institutions, cultural institutions, and interpretation centres? And how can these be designed at the architectural, urban-design and urban-planning scales?

Given the high degree of institutional and bureaucratic overlaps in administering and planning for these monuments

and garden sites within Agra, what collaborations and synergies might encourage deeper coordination and economic integration of these sites at different geographic and governance scales? The specific sites or scales for consideration could be at one end of the spectrum, the 6-kilometre stretch of the Yamuna within the city of Agra and along the heritage landscape of the Taj Mahal and its adjoining monuments. At the other end of the spectrum could be the larger city of Agra, its hinterland, and outwards, the broader geography of the sacred sites in Uttar Pradesh. Additionally, there could be an integrated plan for the riverfront and potential of connecting prime heritage sites back into the life of the city, exploring the possible reuse of certain fallow sites along the riverfront for the land, and people adjacent to heritage sites. India has much to gain in the immediate and longer-term future by promoting integrated approaches to conservation planning for these high-visibility and important heritage sites.

Naturally, an extension of this approach would be to think about the larger economic, historical and cultural landscape in which the Taj Mahal and Agra are more broadly located.

Above: The buffer zones to protect the Taj Mahal are a classic case in point where the stricter the buffer zones, the more isolated is the city from the monuments as then the monuments secede to an abstract entity or authority. Monuments require context and meaning as much as relevance in the present.

Above and top: View of the Fatehbad courtyard after the restoration by the ASI in collaboration with the TMCC. The arcades were restored with the adjoining rooms for an exhibition on the Taj Mahal as part of the visitor facilities. Restoration was completed in 2008.

Imagining a heritage route which includes Vrindavan and Mathura as part of the imaginary of tourist development will create a more stable tourism economy for the future and break the travel operator nexus with the Tourism Department that promotes the idea of Agra as a day trip! This, in turn, influences government policy through infrastructure investments to turn tourists around in 12 hours from Delhi through a quick immersion at the Taj Mahal and Agra Fort – an itinerary that spells disaster for the economy of Agra, and ensures that very little trickles down to the local community. In an announcement in the *Times of India*, Agra on 4 July 2014, Delhi to Agra travel time would be down to 90 minutes in 2015 – only exacerbating the drain on Agra's economy, or put another way – isolating the Taj Mahal from the economic benefits for the citizens of Agra.

Thus, a counter imagination that sees the Taj Mahal as part of the ecology of Agra and then sees Agra as part of a broader ecology that includes Vrindavan and Mathura and perhaps a pan-Uttar Pradesh tourist geography would be a far more robust imagination as the basis of policy and investment from the State to prop up the health of Agra and its incredible heritage sites.

INCOMPARABLE HERITAGE

In 2006 (May 20, *Times of India*), when India's first environmental policy was announced, it resonated some critical concerns for the conservation of the Taj Mahal. The policy introduced the concept of 'incomparable value'. The examples cited were the Taj Mahal, the Tiger and the unique landscape of the Valley of Flowers. The policy articulated 'entities such as these that fit the bill will have to be identified'. The report on the policy went on to state, 'that in these cases, there was a clear consensus that (for them to survive) the (broader) ecosystem should not be disturbed.' The policy also included a definition saying that these 'entities would have priority in the allocation of societal and economic resources for their conservation without consideration of direct or immediate economic benefit.' The central issues in the policy were to do with livelihood issues, which should be used to make and facilitate the protection of this incomparable heritage. For example, the policy was against implicit and explicit subsidies for water and power, fertiliser and pesticides. The policy also discouraged non-metered power supply to farmers, detailing the impact of power-pricing on groundwater use. It encourages partnerships and the involvement of the private sector in management, for instance, in sewage treatment, landfills, and environmental monitoring. It states that environmental standards have to be tailored to the economic and social development situations in which they apply. The stated dominant theme in the policy is that while resources must be conserved to secure livelihood and the well-being of all, the best way to do this is to ensure people, dependent on particular resources, get better livelihood from conservation rather than degradation.

At a time when economic growth seems to be the driving concern for politics in India, this declaration was a welcome piece of policy formulation, albeit not something that has been consciously implemented by Government in the last decade. Clearly, in the case of the Tiger and the Valley of Flowers, there is absolutely no contestation about the fact that their broader ecologies are critical to their survival. However, in the case of the Taj Mahal, this issue is never discussed. Perhaps, because monuments as static entities, are perceived as being self-sufficient, and isolating them is seen as the simplest way to deal with their preservation. On the contrary, for monuments like the Taj Mahal, this broader consensus on the environment it is set in is crucial to taking forward any strategy for its conservation. In fact, the health of the ecology that the monuments are situated in is as crucial as the monument itself – an ecology that consists of social networks and cultural as well as natural systems that have to coexist in synergy for the system to stay balanced. It is in this context that focusing on the health of Agra becomes once again an important question in the discussion about the Taj Mahal and its future imagination. And it is here that the 'Multiple Narratives' hold the potential to connect the monument through the many stories that surround it to the broader community it is set in – the community of Agra residents, the tourists who come from other parts of India and the global travellers who visit this World Heritage Site. It is the simultaneous surfacing of narratives that connect all these constituencies that will, we hope, be the first step in embedding the monument in its context, and in helping establish both contemporary as well as historic narratives which will meld into a robust mesh to sustain not only the Taj Mahal but Agra, a mesh that is inclusive and one that sets up protocol and processes that bring together conservation and planning not as contradictory but rather supplementary enterprises; an approach that is founded on the idea that the future of the Taj Mahal is, after all, intrinsically linked to the future of the city of Agra.

Below and bottom: Views of the exterior of the Fatehbad courtyard after restoration. This space was proposed as a visitor facilities during the partnership between the NCF, ASI and IHCL.

Endnotes

Introduction: Multiple Narratives

1. *The Art Bulletin*, 61(1972) 7-37.
2. Barrucand, Marianne, 'The Garden as a Reflection of Paradise,' *Islam: Art and Architecture, Hattstien and Delius*, Konemann, 2004, p. 490.
3. Roman Transliteration of the Holy Qur'an (with full Arabic text). English translation by Abdullah Yusuf Ali; published by Sh. Muhamad Ashraf, Lahore Pakistan, 1934.

1 Building the Riverfront City

1. Smith, V.A., *Oxford History of India* (third edition), Clarendon Press, Oxford, 1961, p. 321.
2. *Baburnama: Memoirs of Babur Prince and Emperor*, translated, edited and annotated by Wheeler M. Thackston, Oxford University Press in association with the Freer Gallery of Art and Arthur M. Sackler Gallery, New York, 1996 (1504-05) 167-170.
3. *Ibid.*, p. 334.
4. *Ibid.*, p. 333.
5. *Ibid.*, p. 351.
6. *Ibid.*, p. 351.
7. *Ibid.*, pp. 359-360.
8. *Ibid.*, p. 360.
9. Crowe, Sylvia, Sheila Haywood, Susan Jellicoe, and Gordon Patterson, *The Gardens of Mughal India*, Vikas Publishing House Pvt Ltd, Delhi, 1973, p. 66.
10. *Ibid.*, p. 66.
11. Gascoigne, B., *The Great Mughals*, Jonathan Cape, London, 1971, p. 99.
12. *Ibid.*, p. 54.
13. Ralph Fitch in Nath, R., *Agra and its Monumental Glory*, Taraporevala, Bombay, 1977, Contemporary Accounts of the Metropolis of Agra, pp. 12-15.
14. Abul Fazl in Nath, R., *Agra and its Monuments*; The Historical Research Documentation Programme, Medieval Character of the City, 1997, pp. 159-162.
15. Monserrate, A., *The Commentary of Father Monserrate SJ on His Journey to the Court of Akbar*: translated by J. Hoyland, Oxford, Oxford Unversity Press, 1922, p. 36.
16. J.B. Tavernier in Preston, D. and M., *A Teardrop on the Cheek of Time*, Doubleday, London, 2007, p. 139.
17. Nicoll, F., *Shah Jahan: The Rise and Fall of the Mughal Emperor*, Penguin Viking, New Delhi, 2009, p. 33.
18. William Finch in Nath, R., *Agra and its Monumental Glory*, *op. cit.*, pp. 12-15.
19. Lall, J. and D.N. Dube, *Taj Mahal and the Glory of Mughal Agra*, Lustre Press, Varanasi, 1982, p. 96.
20. Nicoll, F., *op. cit.*, p. 155.
21. Preston, D. and M., *op. cit.*, p. 126.
22. François Bernier in Nath, R., *Agra and its Monumental Glory*, *op. cit.*, p. 15.
23. Preston, D. and M., *op. cit*, p. 136.
24. Pelsaert, F., W.H. Moreland and P. Geyle (tr.) *Jahangir's India: The Remonstrantie of Francisco Pelsaert*, Cambridge, W.Heffer and Sons, 1925, pp 162-4.
25. Westcoat, J., and Wolschke Bulman, *Mughal Gardens: Sources, Places, Representation and Prospect*, Dumbarton Oaks Research Library and Collection, Washington, 1996, p. 25.
26. Petroculli, A., *Rethinking the Islamic Garden*, Yale School of Forestry and Environmental Studies, Bulletin No. 103, p. 359.

2 Reimagining the Taj

1. Nicoll, F., *op. cit.*, p. 177.
2. Sarkar, J., *Studies in Mughal India*, Kuntaline Press, Calcutta, 1919, pp. 28-29.
3. Begley, W.E., and Z.A.Desai, *Shahjahannama*, Oxford University Press, Delhi, 1990, pp. 70-71.
4. Begley, W.E., and Z.A.Desai, *Taj Mahal: The Illumined Tomb*, The Aga Khan Program for Islamic Architecture, Cambridge, MA, 1989, p. 13.
5. *Ibid.*, p. 41.
6. *Ibid.*, p. 41.
7. Begley, W.E., and Z.A.Desai, *Taj Mahal: The Illumined Tomb*, The Aga Khan Program for Islamic Architecture, Cambridge, MA, 1989, p. 47 – translation of Tabatabai, one of the authors of the *Padshahnama*.
8. *Ibid.*, p. 51.
9. Peter Mundy in Koch, Ebba, *op. cit.*, p. 98.
10. Nicoll, F. *op., cit.*, p. 190.
11. Sura 36 Ya Sin no. 33-35. West Arch, Taj Mahal, tr. Begley and Desai, *Taj Mahal: The Illumined Tomb*, p. 201.
12. Herbert, E.W., *Flora's Empire*, Penguin, Delhi, 2011, p. 216.
13. Tr. by Begley W.E. and Z.A.Desai, *Taj Mahal: The Illumined Tomb*, p. 270.
14. 'The 36th Sura, the Sura Ya Sin, is inscribed on the south, west, north, east arches. The beginning of the Sura is on the southern entrance to the tomb. Verse 36 of this Sura quoted here is on the western side. This Sura is known as 'The Heart of the Quran' and the verse which speaks of the pairs created by God also alludes to non-being and existence, destruction and creation, Noah's flood and its abatement, night and day, darkness and light, the 'death' of the land and its rejuvenation, ignorance and knowledge, and especially to the greatest gift of God, death and life, especially for the righteous and those who have surrendered themselves to God.' Contributed by Raja M.A. Muhamad Khan Mahmoodabad.
15. Begley, W.E., and Z.A.Desai, *Taj Mahal The Illumined Tomb*, The Aga Khan Program for Islamic Architecture, Cambridge, MA, 1989, p. 67.
16. *Ibid.*, Sura 89, 27, 28, 29, 30, p. 195.
17. *Ibid.*, p. 66.
18. *Ibid.*, p. 74.
19. Tavernier, J.B., *Travels in India*, (tr.) V. Ball, in Kanwar, H.I.S., Unpublished Report, ASI Library, Delhi, 1972.

3 Crafting The Taj

1. Nicoll, F., *op. cit.*, p. 192.
2. Bikaner State Archives, S.N. 27. Also Begley, W.E., and Z.A.Desai, *Taj Mahal: The Illumined Tomb*, The Aga Khan Program for Islamic Architecture, Cambridge, MA, 1989, pp. 163-165.

3. Begley, W.E., and Z.A.Desai, *Taj Mahal: The Illumined Tomb*, The Aga Khan Program for Islamic Architecture, Cambridge, MA, 1989, pp. 163-165.

4. Bhat, P.S., and A.L. Athawale, 'The Question of the Taj Mahal' (from *Itihas Patrika*, Vol. 5, pp. 98-111, 1985).

5. Kanwar, H.I. S., *op. cit.*

6. *Ibid.*

7. Nath, R., *Taj Mahal and Its Incarnation*, The Historical Research and Documentation Program, Jaipur, 1985.

8. Begley, W.E., and Z.A.Desai, *Taj Mahal: The Illumined Tomb*, The Aga Khan Program for Islamic Architecture, Cambridge, MA, 1989, p. 66.

9. Kanwar, H.I S., *op. cit.*

10. Lahauri in Koch, Ebba, *op. cit.*, p. 170.

11. Nicoll, F., *op. cit.*, p. 196.

12. Begley, W.E., and Z.A. Desai, *Taj Mahal: The Illumined Tomb*, The Aga Khan Program for Islamic Architecture, Cambridge, MA, 1989, p. 80.

13. Moynihan, E., *The Moonlight Garden*, Arthur M. Sackler Gallery, Smithsonian Institution in association with the University of Washington, Seattle and London, 2000, p. 28.

4 Changing Urban Landscapes

1. François Bernier in Nath, R., *Agra And Its Monumental Glory, op. cit.*, p. 15.

2. Princep, Val. C., *Imperial India: An Artist's Journals, 1876-77*, Chapman and Hall, London, 1879, reprint Asian Education Services, New Delhi, 2011, p. 60.

3. Caroll, D., *Newsweek*, New York, 1972.

4. *Ibid.*

5. Rousselet, L., *India and its Native Princes, Travels in Central India and the Presidencies of Bombay and Bengal*, first published London, 1875, reprint Asian Educational Services, Delhi, 2006, p. 274.

6. *Ibid.*, p. 275.

7. Princep, Val. C., *op. cit.*, p. 61.

8. *Ibid.*, p. 61.

9. Herbert, E.W., *op. cit.*, p. 198.

10. Curzon in Grewal, R., *In the Shadow of the Taj*, Penguin, Delhi, 2007, p. 241.

11. Fanny Parks in Herbert, E.W., *op. cit.*, p. 203.

12. Dilks, D., *Curzon in India*, Vol. 1, Rupert Hart Davis, London, 1969, p. 245 notating Raleigh, p. 20.

13. *Ibid.*, p. 20.

14. Dilks, D., *op. cit.*, p. 246.

15. *Newsweek*, New York, 1972.

16. *Ibid.*

17. Curzon in Preston, D., and M., *op. cit.*, p. 294.

18. J.H. Marshall in Herbert, E.W., *op. cit.*, p. 203.

19. For full judgement, see M.C. Mehta *vs* the State on the Internet. https://indiankanoon.org/doc/1964392/

Epilogue: The Future of the Taj Mahal

1. Khosla, Renu, 'Agra's Street Culture' in SEMINAR 657, May 2014, p. 50.

Picture Credits

Bibliography

Archer, Mildred, *Early Views of India: The Picturesque Journey of Thomas and William Daniell, 1786-1794*, Thames and Hudson, UK, 1980.

Barrucand Marianne, *The Garden as a Reflection of Paradise; Islam Art and Architecture*, Hattstien and Dellius, Konemann, 2004.

Begley, W.E., and Z.A. Desai, *Taj Mahal: The Illumined Tomb*, Cambridge: The Aga Khan Program for Islamic Architecture, Harvard University Art Museums, 1989.

———— (Eds.), *The Shahjahanama*, Oxford University Press, Delhi 1990.

Carlyle, A.C.L., 'Cunningham Report,' Archaeological Survey of India Report, Vol. IV, ASI Library, 1871-72.

Carroll, David, *Newsweek*, 'The Taj Mahal and its Incarnation,' New York, 1972.

Crowe, Sylvia, Sheila Haywood, Susan Jellicoe, and Gordon Patterson, *The Gardens of Mughal India*, Vikas Publishing House Pvt. Ltd., London, 1973.

Currim, Mumtaz, *Jannat: Paradise in Islamic Art*, The Marg Foundation, Mumbai, 2012.

Das, Ashok Kumar, *Wonders of Nature: Ustad Mansur at the Mughal Court*, The Marg Foundation, Mumbai, 2012.

Desai, Z.A., and H.K. Kaul, *Taj Musem*, Archaeological Survey of India, New Delhi, 1982.

Dilks, David, *Curzon in India*, Vol. 1, Rupert Hart Davis, London, 1969.

Edensor, Tim, *Tourists at the Taj*, Routledge, London, 1998.

Flores, Jorge, and Vassalla e Silva Nuno, *Goa and the Great Mughal*, Calouste Gulbenkian Foundation, Lisbon, 2004.

Gascoigne, Bamber, *The Great Mughals*, Jonathan Cape, London, 1971.

Grewal, Royina, *In the Shadow of the Taj: A Portrait of Agra*, Penguin Books India, New Delhi, 2007.

Herbert, Eugenia W., *Flora's Empire*, University of Pennsylvania Press, Philadelphia, 2011.

Harkness, Terence, and Amita Sinha, 'Taj Heritage Corridor: Intersections Between History and Culture on the Yamuna Riverfront,' College of Environmental Design, University of California, Berkeley, 2004.

Havel, E.B., *Handbook to Agra and the Taj*, Sagar Publications, 1970.

Indian Archaeology, A Review, ASI, New Delhi,1958-59.

J.S. Hoyland and S.N. Banerjee, *The Commentary of Father Monserrate On His Journey to the Court of Akbar*, OUP London 1922; reprint Asian Educational Services, Delhi 2003.

Kanwar, H.I.S., *Taj Mahal: the Most Fabulous Tomb on Earth*, ASI Library, Delhi, 1974.

Keyserling, Count Hermann A., *Indian Travel: Diary of a Philosopher*, Bhavan's Book University, Bombay, 1959.

Keene, H.G., *Handbook for Visitors to Agra and its Neighbourhood*, 1873, Calcutta 5th edition, 1899 Thacker Spink & Co., Agra, 1878.

Khan, Shahena, Dissertation: 'Rediscovering and presenting Moghul Agra to redirect the integrated process of development along the Yamuna riverfront of Mughal Agra,' School of Planning and Architecture, Architectural Conservation, Delhi, 2007.

Koch, Ebba, *Mughal Architecture*, Prestel, Munich, 1991.

————, *The Complete Taj Mahal*, Bookwise (India) Pvt. Ltd., New Delhi, 2006.

Latif, Syad Muhammad, *Agra – Historical and Descriptive*: With an Account of Akbar and His Court and of the Modern City of Agra, 1896.

Lane-Smith, Ron, *The Taj Mahal of Agra*, Stonehenge, New Delhi, 1999.

Lall, John, *Taj Mahal and the Saga of the Great Mughals*, Lustre Press, New Delhi, 1996.

Lall, John and J.N. Dube, *Taj Mahal and the Garden of Mughal Agra*, Lustre Press, Varanasi, 1982.

Lehrman, Jonas B., *Earthly Paradise: Garden and Courtyard in Islam*, Thames and Hudson, UK, 1980.

MARG, 'Gardens of the Great Mughals,' Vol. XXVI, No 1, Dec. 1972, Bombay.

Moynihan, Elizabeth B., *The Moonlight Garden: New Discoveries at the Taj Mahal*, Arthur M. Sackler Gallery, Smithsonian Institution, Washington D.C., 2000.

Michell, George, *Mughal Style: The Art and Architecture of Islamic India*, India Book House, Mumbai, 2007.

Khullar, Reeta, and Rupinder Khullar, *Taj Mahal & Agra: Legacy of the Great Mughals*, Frontline Books, New Delhi, 2010.

Khullar, Rupinder, *501 Images of Taj Mahal and Glimpses of Mughal Agra*, Pictak Books, New Delhi, 1997.

Mishra, Manjari, 'For 12 years, marooned around Taj, villages leading a no-vehicle life.' *The Times of India*, March 4, 2011.

Nath, R., *The Immortal Taj Mahal – the Evolution of the Tomb in Moghul Architecture*, D.B. Taraporevala Sons & Co. Pvt. Ltd., Bombay, 1972.

———, *Agra and its Monumental Glory*, Taraporevala Sons & Co. Pvt. Ltd., Bombay, 1977.

———, 'The Taj Mahal and its Incarnation,' The Historical Research and Documentation Programme, Jaipur, 1985.

———, 'Agra and its Monuments,' The Historical Research and Documentation Programme, 1997.

———, *Art & Architecture of the Taj Mahal*, Historical Research Documentation Programme, Agra, 1996.

———, *History of Mughal Architecture,* 4 Vols., Abhinav Delhi, 2005

———, *Fatehpur Sikri and its Monuments*, Historical Research Documentation Programme, Agra, 2000.

———,Nicoll, Fergus, *Shah Jahan: The Rise and Fall of the Mughal Emperor*, Penguin Viking, New Delhi, 2009.

Okada, Amina, and Joshi, M.C., *Taj Mahal*, Imprimerie Nationale Editions, Paris, 1993.

Peck, Lucy, *Agra: The Architectural Heritage*, Roli Books, Delhi, 2008.

Petroccioli, Attillio Muqarnas, 'Gardens in the Time of Great Empires,' Journal of the Agha Khan Program for Islamic Studies, Vol. VII, E.J. Brill, Leiden, 1997.

Pal, Pratapaditya, Janice Leoshko, Stephen Markel and Joseph M. Dye, *Romance of the Taj Mahal*, Thames & Hudson, New York, 1989.

Preston, Diana, and Michael Preston, *Taj Mahal: Passion and Genius at the Heart of the Moghul Empire*, Preston Writing Partnership, New York, 2007.

———, *A Teardrop on the Cheek of Time*, Doubleday, UK, 2007.

Princep, Val. C., *Imperial India, An Artist's Journal, 1876-1877* (National Archives of India, Delhi); reprint Asian Educational Services, Delhi, 2011.

Rai, Raghu, *Taj Mahal*, Times Book International, Delhi, 1989.

Rezavi, Syed Ali Nadeem, *Fatehpur Sikri Revisited*, Oxford University Press, Delhi, 2013.

Rousselet, Louis, *India and its Native Princes, Travels in Central India and the Presidencies of Bombay and Bengal.* First published, London, 1875; reprint Asian Educational Services, Delhi, 2006.

Siddiqi, W.H., *Taj Mahal,* Archaeological Survey of India, New Delhi, 2009.

Smith, Vincent A., *Oxford History of India,* Oxford University Press, London, 1958.

Taj Mahal Conservation Collaborative Briefing Document, 2001. Unpublished, Pvt.

Taj Mahal Conservation Collaborative Site Management Plan, 2003. Unpublished, Pvt.

Tillotson, Giles, *Taj Mahal*, Harvard University Press, Cambridge, 2008.

Thackston, Wheeler (ed.), *Baburnama*, Smithsonian Institution and Oxford University Press, New York, 1996.

———, *Padshahnama, King of the World*—published for the exhibition 'King of the World' based on the Mughal Manuscript from the Royal Library, Windsor, edited by Ebba Koch and Milo C. Beach, Azimuth Editions Ltd., London, 1997.

———, *Jahangirnama*, Smithsonian Institution and Oxford University Press, New York, 1999.

U.P. District Gazetteer, Agra, 1905.

U.P. District Gazetteer, Agra, 1965.

Villiers-Stuart, Constance Mary, *Gardens of the Great Mughals*, A&C Black, London, 1913.

Westcoat, James and Bulman, Joachim Wokschke, 'Mughal Gardens, Sources Places, Representations, and Prospects,' – papers presented at the 16th Dumbarton Oaks Colloquium on 'History of Landscape Architecture' in collaboration with the Arthur M. Sackler Gallery, Washington D.C., 1992.

Westcoat, James and Rehman, Hussain Mahmood Andul, *The Mughal Garden: Interpretation, Conservation and Implications*; Ferozsons Ltd., Lahore, 1996.

Wilbur, Donald N., *Persian Gardens and Garden Pavilions,* Tuttle, UK, 1962.

Wheeler, Mortimer, *Splendours of the East*, Hamlyn, UK, 1970.

Glossary

abshar-i-chadari	sheet-like waterfall
amrudi shakl	guava-shaped
anar	pomegranate
andhi	dust storm particular to north India
anjir	fig
badam	almond
bagh	garden
bangla	roof-style with eaves, originally from Bengal
Bengal baradari pavilions	twelve-doored pavilion; twelve-pillared
burj	usually fort towers
chabutra	platform
chaddar	sheet
char bagh	garden divided into four quarters by canals, each having pathways, with a tank, pavilion or building at the centre point
chaukandi	four-pillared pavilion; four-sided pavilion; also *chaukhandi*
chhattri	small-domed pavilion
choubdar	gatekeeper; armed guard
chunam	lime plaster
darajat-i-daqaiq	degrees of accuracy; high esteem
darbar	royal audience
dargah	shrine of a Sufi saint
darwaza	gate; door
farma	stencil
firdaus	paradise
firman	imperial orders
gajyavala	panel displaying the surrender of seven elephants to a mythical beast
gaz	unit of measure; one yard
ghat	buildings with waterfront steps
guldasta	vase
hafiz	one who recites the Quran by heart
hamman	bathhouse, bathroom or bathing complex contained in an independent building
haram	forbidden by Islamic law; also harem, in the present context
hasht bihisht	'Eight Paradises'; refers to a Timurid palace building type consisting of two storeys of four corner rooms around a central domed space
imbli	tamarind
iwan	central arched entrance or portal originally with barrel-vaulted ceiling; archway in the centre of a building's façade; in Mughal buildings, it is rectangular or semi-octagonal with a semi-soffit or vaulted ceiling; distinct from *aiwan* which is a hall or *dalan*
jagir	property
jali	screen
jammat khana	place or building where people assemble, usually for religious discourses or worship
jamun	purple-coloured Indian summer fruit; black plum; java plum
jannat	eternal place
jawab	answer; response; possibly 'reflection' in the present context
jilau khana	colonnaded *dalans** with chambers on all sides at the approach of a palace or mausoleum, to provide a setting and monumental introduction; **dalan* (cloister): three-sided verandah in an Indian mosque; covered passage round an open court
kachnar	Bauhinia
kalash	ancient Indian water-pot; integral part of the Mughal finial used to crown the domes and cupolas of *chhattris*, composed of discs and a water-pot

karigar	craftsman
katra	bylane
khadim	domestic servant or slave; servant who has charge of a tomb or mosque
khajur	date (fruit)
khattu	gold-coloured marble
khwasspura	servants' quarter attached to a palace or mausoleum
kos	unit of land; distance varying from 1 to 3 miles
kumhaar	potter
kursi	chair
loha	iron
mahal	palace
mahapadma	sheath of 6, 8, 12, 16, 24 or 32 stylised lotus petals carved in stone or stucco, surmounting the dome; a distinctive feature of Indian domes
mandi	marketplace
mehman khana	guest house
mihrab	niche or marker, usually used to indicate the direction of prayer in a mosque
mishqual	a medieval measurement
mutawatir	consecutively reported, traced by a perfect chronological chain of ascertained narrators of the Hadith
mutsaddi	post for executive officials in Mughal India
na mahram	stranger; outsider; untrustworthy person
nashpati	pear
naubat khana	gateway where *naubat* or ceremonial music is performed at fixed hours; also called *naqqar khana* though the former is more ceremonial and auspicious in character than the latter
omrah	nobleman at the court of the emperor
pada	locality
parchin kari	art of inlay; inlaying
peshkash	present; tribute
pietra dura	highly polished Florentine mosaic of *lapis lazuli* and marble
pishtaq	Iranian term for a portal projecting from a building's façade
purdah	curtain; practice of segregating women from men or strangers, especially by means of a curtain
qanat	series of well-like vertical shafts, connected by gently sloping tunnels
rauza	Persian term for mausoleum
saib	apple
serai	Persian term for travellers' resting place; also *caravanserai*
shahtut	Indian mulberry; also called King mulberry
swastika	Sanskrit word for 'It is' or well-being; auspicious Hindu symbol
takht	platform; podium; throne
tal	tank; reservoir
tarbooz	watermelon
tehkhana	basement; underground chamber or vault
tola	old Indian unit of weight
ulema	Muslim scholars with in-depth knowledge of Islam
umma	nation/community bound together by religion
urs	death anniversary of a saintly person, celebrating the union of the soul with God
waqf	trust for Islamic properties
zamini	landed
zenana	harem; women's quarters

Index